As "cover girl," officer manager of Bon Vivant Press

and owner of authors Robert and Kathleen Fish,

I would like to share the joys of our vacations and working

trips to produce our *Cooking Secrets* series.

This book is dedicated in loving memory of my bon vivant

canine pal, Rugen.

— *Dreamer Dawg*

AMERICA'S SOUTH EDITION

Pets Welcome

A Guide to Hotels, Inns, and Resorts That Welcome You and Your Pet

KATHLEEN AND ROBERT FISH

BON VIVANT

Library of Congress Cataloging-in-Publication Data
Pets Welcome™ America's South
A Guide to Hotels, Inns and Resorts That Welcome You and Your Pet
Fish, Kathleen DeVanna
97-071559
ISBN 1-883214-17-3
$15.95 softcover
Includes indexes

Cover photography by Robert N. Fish
Editorial direction by Charlotte D. Atkins and Judie Marks
Editorial assistance by Susan Parkes
Cover design by Morris Design
Illustrations by Krishna Gopa, Graphic Design & Illustration and
Gerrica Connolly, Design Studio
Type by Cimarron Design

Published by Bon Vivant Press
a division of The Millennium Publishing Group
P.O. Box 1994
Monterey, CA 93942

Printed in the United States of America
by Publishers Press

Contents

Abbreviations Used in this Book

AAA   American Automobile Association
ABA   American Breeders Association
AKC   American Kennel Club
AARP American Association of Retired Persons

Introduction

T raveling with people we love and whose company we enjoy can be one of life's great pleasures. Our pets can be counted among those who enrich our lives. So it is little wonder that more than 40 million of us choose to take our pets along with us when we travel.

Hundreds of hotels, inns, guest ranches and bed and breakfasts throughout America's South welcome pets with open arms. Of course, just as they each offer different amenities and accommodations, they also have a wide range of pet policies.

That's why *Pets Welcome*™ will be a handy resource for you, to help you discover and select some of the best places to stay when traveling with your four-legged companions. We have researched and ranked a broad spectrum of places, from romantic hideaways to inns that have made a trademark name for themselves in the hospitality industry.

Each hotel or inn was chosen because of its ambiance, special charm, guest amenities and, of course, its pet friendliness. We have bestowed each with our three-, four- or five-paw designation.

In addition, original pen-and-ink artist's renderings share a glimpse of each place's awaiting character and charm.

We have included lodging that should meet all types of travel needs and budgets, from luxurious and romantic or high-tech and convenient to secluded and quirky or warm and rustic.

In addition to the accommodation summaries, this guidebook provides maps and details on points of interest throughout America's South, including parks, beaches and points of interest.

Whether you and your pet are travel veterans or setting out on a trip together for the first time, you'll no doubt learn a valuable lesson or two from the travel tips provided by the Humane Society of the United States. These helpful hints offer insight into traveling by car, plane and other modes of transportation, and offer specialized guidance on crating animals, documentation, basic care and courtesy information.

It is our hope that as you travel throughout the South, you will return time and time again to this book as you would to your favorite inn—finding comfort in knowing that the places found within welcome both you and your pet, that details are both useful and intriguing and that it can open doors to new and exciting adventures. In fact, we hope you use it so much that it becomes, well, dog-eared.

Top Ten Travel Tips

1 Bring your pet's own food, dishes, litter and litter box, leash, collar with ID tags, a first aid kit and a bottle of water from home. This will make your pet more comfortable, prepare you for emergencies and decrease the chances of an upset stomach from a strange brand of food. Maintain the normal feeding and walking schedule as much as possible. Be sure to bring old bath towels or paper towels in case of an accident and plastic bags to dispose of your pet's waste. It is a good idea to bring a picture of your pet for identification purposes in case you and your pet become separated.

2 Bring your pet's vaccination records with you when traveling in state, and a health certificate when traveling out of state. If you plan on boarding him at anytime during your vacation, call the boarding kennel to reserve his space, see what they require you to bring and if they require a health certificate.

3 Bring your pet's favorite toys, leash, grooming supplies, medications and bedding. It is a good idea to bring an old sheet or blanket from home to place over the hotel's bedding, just in case your pet gets on the bed. It will also come in handy to protect your car seats from hair and dirty paws.

4 Tape the address of where you are staying on the back of your pet's ID tag or add a laminated card or new ID tag to your pet's collar, or add a second collar with a friend or family members phone number. This information is also good to have on your pet's collar in case of a natural disaster so that someone out of your area can be contacted if you and your pet become separated.

5 Do not leave your pets unattended in a hotel room. The surroundings are new and unfamiliar to your animal and may cause him to become upset and destroy property he normally would not or bark excessively and disturb your neighbors. You also run the risk of his escaping. If a maid should open the door to clean your room, the pet may see this as a chance to find you and escape, or worse, he may attack the maid out of fear.

6 Train your pet to use a crate. This will come in handy if you ever need to travel by plane. Make sure the crate has enough room for your pet to stand up comfortably and turn around inside. Be sure to trim your pet's nails so that they don't get caught in the crate door or ventilation holes. Crates come in handy in hotel rooms, too. If your pet is already used to being in a crate, he will not object if you leave him in one long enough for you to go out to breakfast. Never take your pet with you if you will have to leave him in the car. If it is 85 degrees outside, within minutes the inside of the car can reach over 160 degrees, even with the windows cracked, causing heat stroke and possible death. According to The Humane Society of the United States, the signs of heat stress are: heavy panting, glazed eyes, a rapid pulse, unsteadiness, a staggering gait, vomiting, or a deep red or purple tongue. If heat stroke does occur, the pet must be cooled by dousing him with water and applying ice packs to his head and neck. He should then be taken to a veterinarian immediately.

7 When your pet is confined to a crate, the best way to provide water for your pet is to freeze water in the cup that hooks onto the door of your pet's crate. This way they will get needed moisture without the water splashing all over the crate. Freezing water in your pet's regular water bowl also works well for car trips.

8 Be sure to put your pet's favorite toys and bedding in the crate. Label the crate with "LIVE ANIMAL" and "THIS END UP," plus the address and phone number of your destination, as well as your home address and phone number and the number of someone to contact in case of an emergency.

9 When traveling by plane, be sure to book the most direct flights possible. The less your pet has to be transferred from plane to plane, the less chance of your being separated. This is also important when traveling in hot or cold weather. You don't want your pet to have to wait in the cargo hold of a plane or be exposed to bad weather for any longer than necessary. Check with airlines for the type of crate they require and any additional requirements. They are very strict about the size and type of crate you may carry on board.

10 Do not feed your pet before traveling. This reduces the risk of an upset stomach or an accident in his crate or your car. When traveling by car, remember that your pet needs rest stops as often as you do. It is a good idea for everyone to stretch their legs from time to time. If your pet is unfamiliar with car travel, then get him use to the car gradually. Start a few weeks before your trip with short trips around town and extend the trips a little each time. Then he will become accustomed to the car before your trip and it will be more pleasant for all involved.

Traveling With Your Pet

Courtesy of The Humane Society of the United States (HSUS)
2100 "L" Street, N.W.
Washington, D.C. 20037

 If you are planning a trip and you share your life with a pet, you have a few decisions to make before you set off. The following are tips to help you plan a safer and smoother trip for both you and your pet.

SHOULD YOU TRAVEL WITH YOUR PET?

Some pets are not suited for travel because of temperament, illness or physical impairment. If you have any doubts about whether it is appropriate for your pet to travel, talk to your veterinarian.

If you decide that your pet should not travel with you, consider the alternatives: Have a responsible friend or relative look after your pet, board your pet at a kennel or hire a sitter to visit, feed and exercise your pet.

If a friend or relative is going to take care of your pet, ask if that person can take your pet into his or her home. Animals can get lonely when left at home alone. Be sure your pet is comfortable with his or her temporary caretaker and any pets that person has.

If you choose to board your pet, get references and inspect the kennel. Your veterinarian or local shelter can help you select a facility. If you are hiring a sitter, interview the candidates and check their references. (A pet sitter may be preferable if your pet is timid or elderly and needs the comfort of familiar surroundings during your absence.)

Whatever option you choose, there are a few things to remember. Your pet should be up-to-date on all vaccinations and in sound health. Whoever is caring for your pet should know the telephone number at which you can be reached, the name and telephone number of your veterinarian and your pet's medical or dietary needs. Be sure your pet is comfortable with the person you have chosen to take care of him or her.

If You Plan to Travel with Your Pet

THE PRE-TRIP VETERINARY EXAMINATION

Before any trip, have your veterinarian examine your pet to ensure that he or she is in good health. A veterinary examination is a requisite for obtaining legal documents required for many forms of travel.

In addition to the examination, your veterinarian should provide necessary vaccinations such as rabies, distemper, infectious hepatitis and leptospirosis. If your pet is already up-to-date on these, obtain written proof.

Your veterinarian may prescribe a tranquilizer for the pet who is a nervous traveler; however, such drugs should be considered only after discussion with your veterinarian. He or she may recommend a trial run in which your pet is given the prescribed dosage so you can observe the effects. Do not give your pet any drug not prescribed or given to you by your veterinarian.

LEGAL REQUIREMENTS

When traveling with your pet, it is always advisable to keep a health certificate (a document from your veterinarian certifying that your pet is in good health) and medical records close at hand. If you and your pet will be traveling across state lines, you must obtain from your veterinarian a certificate of rabies vaccination.

Although pets may travel freely throughout the United States as long as they have proper documentation, Hawaii requires a 120-day quarantine for all dogs and cats. Hawaii's quarantine regulations vary by species, so check prior to travel.

If you and your pet are traveling from the United States to Canada, you must carry a certificate issued by a veterinarian that clearly identifies the animal and certifies that the dog or cat has been vaccinated against rabies during the preceding 36-month period. Different Canadian provinces may have different requirements. Be sure to contact the government of the province you plan to visit.

If you and your pet are traveling to Mexico, you must carry a health certificate prepared by your veterinarian within two weeks of the day you cross the border. The certificate must include a description of your pet, the lot number of the rabies vaccine used, indication of distemper vaccination and a veterinarian's statement that the animal is free from infectious or contagious disease. This certificate must be stamped by an office of the U.S. Department of Agriculture (USDA). The fee for the stamp is $4.

Get Ready to Hit the Road

TRAVEL CARRIERS

Travel carriers are useful when your pet is traveling by car; they are mandatory when your pet is traveling by air. Your pet's carrier should be durable and smooth-edged with opaque sides, a grille door and several ventilation holes on each of the four sides. Choose a carrier with a secure door and latch. If you are traveling by air, the carrier should have food and water dishes. Pet carriers may be purchased from pet-supply stores or bought directly from domestic airlines. Select a carrier that has enough room to permit your animal to sit and lie down but is not large enough to allow your pet to be tossed about during travel. You can make the carrier more comfortable by lining the interior with shredded newspaper or a towel. (For air-travel requirements, see the "Traveling by Air" section.)

It is wise to acclimate your pet to the carrier in the months or weeks preceding your trip. Permit your pet to explore the carrier. Place your pet's food dish inside the carrier and confine him or her to the carrier for brief periods.

To introduce your pet to car travel in the carrier, confine him or her in the carrier and take short drives around the neighborhood. If properly introduced to car travel, most dogs and cats will quickly adjust to and even enjoy car trips.

CAREFUL PREPARATION IS KEY

When packing, don't forget your pet's food, food and water dishes, bedding, litter and litter box, leash, collar and tags, grooming supplies and a first aid kit and any necessary medications. Always have a container of drinking water with you.

Your pet should wear a sturdy collar with ID tags throughout the trip. The tags should have both your permanent address and telephone number and an address and telephone number where you or a contact can be reached during your travels.

Traveling can be upsetting to your pet's stomach. Take along ice cubes, which are easier on your pet than large amounts of water. You should keep feeding to a minimum during travel. (Provide a light meal for your pet two or three hours before you leave if you are traveling by car and four to six hours before departure if you are traveling by airplane.) Allow small amounts of water periodically in the hours before the trip.

On Your Way

TRAVELING BY CAR

Dogs who enjoy car travel need not be confined to a carrier if your car has a restraining harness (available at pet-supply stores) or if you are accompanied by a passenger who can restrain the dog. Because most cats are not as comfortable traveling in cars, for their own safety as well as yours, it is best to keep them in a carrier.

Dogs and cats should always be kept safely inside the car. Pets who are allowed to stick their heads out the window can be injured by particles of debris or become ill from having cold air forced into their lungs. Never transport a pet in the back of an open pickup truck.

Stop frequently to allow your pet to exercise and eliminate. Never permit your pet to leave the car without a collar, ID tag and leash.

Never leave your pet unattended in a parked car. On warm days, the temperature in your car can rise to 160 degrees in a matter of minutes, even with the windows opened slightly. Furthermore, an animal left alone in a car is an invitation to pet thieves.

TRAVELING BY AIR

Although thousands of pets fly every year without experiencing problems, there are still risks involved. The Humane Society recommends that you do not transport your pet by air unless absolutely necessary.

If you must transport your companion animal by air, call the airline to check health and immunization requirements for your pet.

If your pet is a cat or a small dog, take him or her on board with you. Be sure to contact airlines to find out the specific requirements for this option. If you pursue this option, you have two choices: Airlines will accept either hard-sided carriers or soft-sided carriers, which may be more comfortable for your pet. Only certain brands of soft sided carriers are acceptable to certain airlines, so call your airline to find out what carrier to use.

If your pet must travel in the cargo hole, you can increase the chances of a safe flight for your pet by following these tips:

- Use direct flights. You will avoid the mistakes that occur during airline transfers and possible delays in getting your pet off of the plane.

- Always travel on the same flight as your pet. Ask the airline if you can watch your pet being loaded and unloaded into the cargo hold.

- When you board the plane, notify the captain and at least one flight attendant that your pet is traveling in the cargo hold. If the captain knows that pets are on board, he or she may take special precautions.

- Do not ship pug-nosed dogs and cats such as Pekinese, Chow Chows and Persians in the cargo hold. These breeds have short nasal passages that leave them vulnerable to oxygen deprivation and heat stroke in cargo holds.

- If traveling during the summer or winter months, choose flights that will accommodate temperature extremes. Early morning or late evening flights are better in the summer; afternoon flights are better in the winter.

- Fit your pet with two pieces of identification—a permanent ID tag with your name and home address and telephone number and a temporary travel ID with the address and telephone number where you or a contact person can be reached.

- Affix a travel label to the carrier, stating your name, permanent address and telephone number and final destination. The label should clearly state where you or a contact person may be reached as soon as the flight arrives.

- Make sure your pet's nails have been clipped to protect against their hooking in the carrier's door, holes and other crevices.

- Give your pet at least a month before your flight to become familiar with the travel carrier. This will minimize his or her stress during travel.

- Your pet should not be given tranquilizers unless they are prescribed by your veterinarian. Make sure your veterinarian understands that this prescription is for air travel.

- Do not feed your pet for four to six hours prior to air travel. Small amounts of water can be given before the trip. If possible, put ice cubes in the water tray attached to the inside of your pet's kennel. A full water bowl will only spill and cause discomfort.

- Try not to fly with your pet during busy travel times such as holidays and summer. Your pet is more likely to undergo rough handling during hectic travel periods.

- Carry a current photo of your pet with you. If your pet is lost during the trip, a photograph will make it easier for airline employees to search effectively.

- When you arrive at your destination, open the carrier as soon as you are in a safe place and examine your pet. If anything seems wrong, take your pet to a veterinarian immediately. Get the results of the examination in writing, including the date and time.

Do not hesitate to complain if you witness the mishandling of an animal—either yours or someone else's—at any airport.

If you have a bad experience when shipping your animal by air, contact The HSUS, the U.S. Department of Agriculture (USDA) and the airline involved. To contact the USDA write to: USDA, Animal, Plant and Health Inspection Service (APHIS), Washington, D.C. 20250.

TRAVELING BY SHIP

With the exception of assistance dogs, only a few cruise lines accept pets—normally only on ocean crossings and frequently confined to kennels. Some lines permit pets in private cabins. Contact cruise lines in advance to find out their policies and which of their ships have kennel facilities. If you must use the ship's kennel, make sure it is protected from the elements.

Follow the general guidelines suggested for other modes of travel when planning a ship voyage.

TRAVELING BY TRAIN

Amtrak currently does not accept pets for transport unless they are assistance dogs. (There may be smaller U.S. railroad companies that permit animals on board their trains.) Many trains in European countries allow pets. Generally, it is the passengers' responsibility to feed and exercise their pets at station stops.

HOTEL ACCOMMODATIONS

There are approximately 8,000 hotel, motels and inns across the United States that accept guests with pets. Most hotels set their own policies, so it is important to call ahead and ask if pets are permitted and if there is a size limit.

IF YOUR PET IS LOST

Whenever you travel with your pet, there is a chance that you and your pet will become separated. It only takes a moment for an animal to stray and become lost. If your pet is missing, immediately canvas the area. Should your pet not be located within a few hours, take the following action:

- Contact the animal control departments and humane societies within a 60-mile radius of where your pet strayed. Check with them each day.

- Post signs at intersections and in store fronts throughout the area.

- Provide a description and a photograph of your missing pet to the police, letter carriers or delivery people.

- Advertise in newspapers and with radio stations. Be certain to list your hotel telephone number on all lost-pet advertisements.

A lost pet may become confused and wary of strangers. Therefore, it may be days, or even weeks, before the animal is retrieved by a Good Samaritan. If you must continue on your trip or return home, arrange for a hotel clerk or shelter employee to contact you if your pet is located.

DO YOUR PART TO MAKE PETS WELCOME GUESTS

Many hotels, restaurants and individuals will give your pet special consideration during your travels. It is important for you to do your part to ensure that dogs and cats will continue to be welcomed as traveling companions. Obey local animal-control ordinances, keep your animal under restraint and be thoughtful and courteous to other travelers.

If you have more specific questions or are traveling with a companion animal other than a dog or cat, contact the Companion Animals section of the HSUS.

HELPFUL HINTS

- To transport birds out of the United States, record the leg-band or tattoo number on the USDA certificate and get required permits from the U.S Fish and Wildlife Service.

- Carry a current photograph of your pet with you. If your pet is lost during a trip, a photograph will make it easier for others (airline employees, the police, shelter workers, etc.) to help find your pet.

- While thousands of pets fly without problems every year, there are risks involved. The HSUS recommends that you do not transport your pet by air unless absolutely necessary.

- Whenever you travel with your pet, there is a chance that you and your pet will be separated. If your pet is lost, immediately canvas the area and take appropriate action.

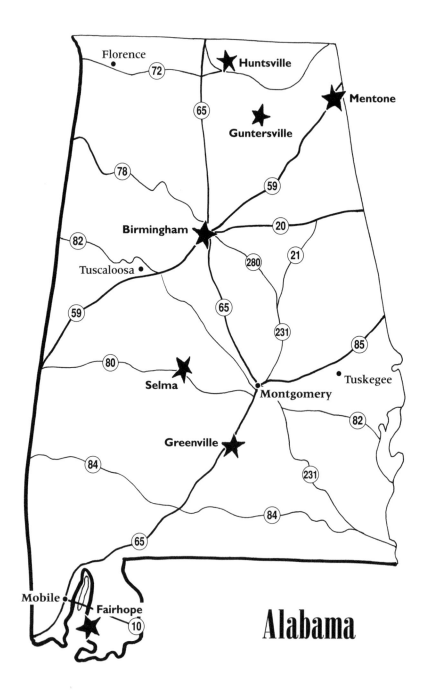

Florence

72

Huntsville

65

Mentone

Guntersville

59

78

Birmingham

20

82

280

21

Tuscaloosa

65

59

231

85

80

Selma

Tuskegee

Montgomery

82

Greenville

231

84

84

65

Mobile

Fairhope

10

Alabama

PETS WELCOME!
Alabama

Tutwiler Hotel

Tutwiler Hotel
2021 Park Place North
Birmingham, AL 35203
800-845-1787 ▪ (205) 322-2100

Room Rates:	$89–$172. AAA, AARP, AKC and ABA discounts. Special packages available.
Pet Charges or Deposits:	None
Rated: 4 Paws 🐾🐾🐾🐾	95 guest rooms and 52 spacious suites furnished with antiques, rich fabrics and marble bathrooms; with complimentary morning paper and shoe shine, health club facilities, 2 award-winning restaurants and cocktail lounge.

A n Alabama tradition since 1914, the award-winning Tutwiler Hotel offers luxury, history and Southern hospitality amid the glass and steel office towers and tourist attractions of Birmingham's vibrant downtown area. History buffs and leisure travelers visit the eight-story red brick building to experience a bygone era when Warren G. Harding was president, Charles Lindbergh was an international hero and Will Rogers was a premier stage performer.

This historic four-star hotel features 147 guest rooms and suites and is furnished with original antiques, intricate masonry work, carved oak chandeliers and original marble tiles. Enjoy an extra touch of luxury on the Heritage Executive Level, featuring a private executive floor with an exclusive lounge for breakfast and cocktails. Guests are invited to take advantage of the health club facilities, where you can work out on state-of-the-art equipment.

Christian's Restaurant is the winner of numerous accolades, including being named among the Top 25 Restaurants in the Country by Best of the Best Dining Awards.

Marcella's Tea Room and Inn

Marcella's Tea Room and Inn
114 Fairhope Avenue
Fairhope, AL 36532
(334) 990-8520

Room Rates: $85–$150, including full breakfast, evening wine and snacks.
Pet Charges or Deposits: $42.50 refundable deposit.
Rated: 4 Paws 🐾🐾🐾🐾   2 guest rooms and a 3-bedroom cottage.

Nestled amid giant, moss-laden live oak trees is the charming town of Fairhope. Located only minutes from Mobile and Pensacola, the town sits atop a scenic bluff overlooking a wide stretch of Mobile Bay. This unforgettable, small Southern town is home to Marcella's Tea Room and Inn. Located just one block from the shops of town, this historical home will entice you to sit a spell on its large, welcoming front porch.

Inside the inn, you will be surrounded by a combination of true Southern hospitality and elegance. A warm atmosphere is prevalent throughout this lovingly decorated home with its antique-filled living and dining rooms, inviting sun room and the two cozy bedrooms with brass and iron beds, lace chintz curtains and private baths.

Your complimentary gourmet breakfast of fresh crêpes with berry sauce, crystal dishes of colorful pears, kiwi and grapes topped with cream sauce, served on heirloom china with sterling silver flatware, will give an elegant start to your day. Be sure to stop by Marcella's Tea Room after your day of sightseeing for a cup of tea. In the evening, guests are invited to enjoy a glass of wine.

Villa Whimsy on Mobile Bay

Villa Whimsy on Mobile Bay
360 South Mobile Street
Fairhope, AL 36532
(334) 928-0226

Room Rates:	$85, including a continental breakfast in your cottage. Mention *Pets Welcome* for a 10% discount.
Pet Charges or Deposits:	None. Manager's approval required.
Rated: 3 Paws ❀❀❀	2 one-bedroom cottages with queen-sized bed and sleeper sofa, private bath, fully equipped kitchen, dining area, separate living area, telephone and television.

I f you are looking for a different type of accommodation in a small Southern town, try the charming and colorful cottages at Villa Whimsy on Mobile Bay. These oak-shaded, one-bedroom cottages are fully furnished with queen-sized beds, full baths, a telephone, cable television, a fully equipped kitchen, dining area, plus the added bonus of a queen sleeper sofa in the living room. These comfortable accommodations provide the perfect atmosphere for a relaxing vacation or weekend retreat.

Guests are invited to fish from the pier, swim in the bay or explore the sandy beaches with their dog.

Holiday Inn

Holiday Inn
941 Fort Dale Road
Greenville, AL 36037
800-HOLIDAY ▪ (334) 382-2651

Room Rates: $52.50–$55. AAA and AARP discounts.
Pet Charges or Deposits: $5 per day. Pets up to 50 lbs.
Rated: 3 Paws 🐾🐾🐾 96 guest rooms with free in-room movies, cable television, some with coffee makers, data ports, valet laundry, swimming pool, restaurant and cocktail lounge.

Conveniently located within a short driving distance of Birmingham, Atlanta or Montgomery, and only 4 miles from Sherling Lake Park—a 125-acre recreation area with a 36-hole golf course, picnic areas, hiking trails, and prime fishing—is the Holiday Inn of Greenville.

Here guests will find a two-story building with exterior corridors, well-kept guest rooms with in-room movies and cable television. The inn offers a large outdoor pool with an area to sunbathe on the surrounding deck. Your dog will appreciate the expansive grounds, a great place for a morning or evening stroll.

Choices Restaurant and the D'Place Lounge are located at the Inn.

Mac's Landing Lodge and Marina

Mac's Landing Lodge and Marina
7001 Val Monte Drive
Guntersville, AL 35976
(205) 582-1000

Room Rates:	$52–$150, including continental breakfast.
Pet Charges or Deposits:	None.
Rated: 3 Paws 🐾🐾🐾	46 guest rooms and 9 suites with kitchenettes, cable television, swimming pool, whirlpool, balconies overlooking the lake or pool, piers, dry dock facilities, full service marina, restaurant and cocktail lounge.

You'll find yourself and your pet on an isolated peninsula, surrounded by the waters of Lake Guntersville, at Mac's Landing Lodge and Marina. Your comfortable accommodations will overlook either the large swimming pool and whirlpool area or the picturesque lake. The tree-lined grounds surrounding the lodge and marina offer plenty of room for you and your dog to stretch your legs or spend the day exploring the 950 miles of shoreline. For those who prefer smaller bodies of water, the lodge has a large swimming pool and whirlpool for guests.

Lake Guntersville flows through the foothills of the Appalachians and is one of the largest man-made lakes in the world. The 69,000-acre lake is fed by the Tennessee River and offers countless opportunities for fishing, boating, water skiing, jet skiing and other water sports. A full-service marina offers wet slips, dry storage facilities, gas docks and the Ship's Store for supplies.

Executive Lodge Suite Hotel

Executive Lodge Suite Hotel
1535 Sparkman Drive
Huntsville, AL 35816
800-248-4722 ▪ (205) 830-8600

Room Rates:	$63–$150, including continental breakfast. AAA, AARP, AKC and ABA discounts.
Pet Charges or Deposits:	$1.50 per day, plus $150 deposit; $120 refundable. Small pets only.
Rated: 3 Paws ❀ ❀ ❀	313 spacious suites with fully equipped kitchens, coffee makers, toasters, Jacuzzi suites, some with ceiling fans, fireplaces, balconies or patios, VCR and movie rentals available, two outdoor pools, laundry facilities and airport transportation.

You no longer have to settle for an ordinary hotel room when you can have a spacious, comfortable suite for the same price. Huntsville's largest suite hotel offers one-, two- and three-bedroom suites and penthouses with all the amenities of home. Suites are tastefully decorated, have fully equipped kitchens with full-size appliances, as well as separate bedroom and living areas. The suites range from 480 square feet of living space for the Studio Suite up to 1,400 square feet of living space, including a balcony, fireplace and Jacuzzi.

Start your day off with the complimentary deluxe continental breakfast, followed by a walk with the dog through the hotel's lovely private park. There are two outdoor swimming pools and free health club privileges to enjoy.

Holiday Inn Space Center

Holiday Inn Space Center
3810 University Drive
Huntsville, AL 35816
800-345-7720 ▪ (205) 837-7171

Room Rates:	$59–$65, including continental breakfast. AAA, AARP and Holiday Inn Priority Club discounts.
Pet Charges or Deposits:	$50 deposit.
Rated: 3 Paws 🐾🐾🐾	112 guest rooms with in-room coffee, hair dryers, irons and boards, large swimming pool, whirlpool, sauna, exercise room, restaurant and cocktail lounge, free airport transportation.

T he Holiday Inn Space Center is conveniently located near Constitution Village, the Von Braun Civic Center and its namesake, the United States Space and Rocket Center.

Guests will appreciate the added convenience of in-room coffee service, hair dryers, and irons and ironing boards. Rooms with small refrigerators and comfortable sofas are also available. A complimentary continental breakfast is included in your room rate.

For those who don't want to miss their regular workout, there is an exercise room. After your workout, relax in the sauna, whirlpool or indoor/outdoor swimming pool.

Ponds Restaurant serves a menu of traditional favorites. If you are looking for a place to meet friends for a cocktail, the hotel's lounge, Hoppers, is a Huntsville hot spot.

Mentone Springs Hotel Bed and Breakfast

Mentone Springs Hotel Bed and Breakfast
6114 Alabama Highway 117
Mentone, AL 35984
(205) 634-4040

Room Rates:	$54–$69, including full breakfast.
Pet Charges or Deposits:	None
Rated: 3 Paws 🐾🐾🐾	9 guest rooms, some with fireplaces and private baths, claw-foot tubs, library room, exercise room, large porch and afternoon tea, resident dog.

Mentone means "musical mountain spring." In 1884, Dr. Frank Caldwell of Pennsylvania visited the local mountain while ill and was restored to health after drinking the mineral spring water. He soon took up permanent residence at Mentone, where he established a health spa called The Mentone Springs Hotel. His first guests came for the curative effects of the mineral springs, to enjoy nature walks and to play croquet on the lawn.

This three-story Queen Anne Victorian has passed through many hands since then. It's now being restored to its original grandeur. Today's guest will find an 1,800-square-foot ballroom, nine guest rooms, some with fireplaces and private baths with claw-foot tubs, and a huge porch where guests may partake of afternoon tea and relax.

For recreation, croquet is still played on the lawn, or you and your dog can venture out to one of the nearby parks. The inn's restaurant, Caldwells, named after the original owner of the inn, is open six days a week.

Grace Hall Bed and Breakfast Inn

Grace Hall Bed and Breakfast Inn
506 Lauderdale Street
Selma, AL 36701
(334) 875-5744

Room Rates:	$69–$99, including full breakfast.
Pet Charges or Deposits:	$10 per stay. Manager's approval required. Small dogs only.
Rated: 5 Paws 🐾🐾🐾🐾🐾	6 guest rooms with private baths, with large courtyard and double parlors. Treats and food are available for pets.

Grace Hall Bed and Breakfast Inn was built in 1857 by Henry Ware and was occupied by the Evans, Baker and Jones families for 110 years. The home was then given to the local Historical Society, which spent five years restoring it to its original grandeur. This ante-bellum mansion mixes elements of the older neoclassicism with the newer Victorian trends. Now on the National Register, Grace Hall is once again a prominent part of the community.

The elegant rooms with crystal chandeliers, wooden plank floors and large oil paintings welcome you to relax by the fire or join in conversation with other guests. This ante-bellum mansion offers six exquisitely decorated guest rooms with private baths, furnished in period antiques, lush draperies, plush upholstery and elegant bedding. Each guest room opens onto the landscaped courtyard.

Alabama

Please Note: *Pets must be on a leash at all times and may be restricted to certain areas. For directions, use fees, pet charges and general information, contact the numbers listed below.*

National Forest General Information

U.S. Forest Service
2946 Chestnut Street
Montgomery, AL 36107

(334) 832-4470 – information
800-280-2267 – reservations

National Forests and Parks

COVINGTON

Conecuh National Forest, located on the Alabama-Florida border, consists of 83,038 acres of forest, with 20 miles of hiking trails along the Conecuh Trail. The park offers camping, fishing, hiking trails, picnic areas, boat ramps for boating and swimming. For more information, call (334) 222-2555.

LAWRENCE AND WINSTON

Bankhead National Forest, located in the towns of Lawrence and Winston in northwestern Alabama, encompasses 179,655 acres. There are beautiful lakes, limestone canyons, a natural bridge, as well as the 25,986-acre Sipsey Wilderness Area, Sipsey River, Corinth Lake, Houston Lake, Brushy Lake and Clear Creek recreation areas. There is abundant wildlife, camping, hiking and bicycling trails, picnic areas, boating and boat ramps, fishing and swimming. For more information, call (205) 489-5111.

TALLADEGA

Talladega National Forest, located in eastern Alabama near the Oakmulgee, southeast of Tuscaloosa, consists of 377,703 acres, divided into two sections. The 45,000-acre Oakmulgee Wildlife Management Area surrounds Payne Lake. The Talladega Division contains two wildlife management areas, the Choccolocco, 39,320 acres, and Hollins, 31,943 acres, and includes the Pinhoti Trail system, which traverses the highest terrain in Alabama with over 100 miles of rugged, scenic country to hike between Chandler Springs and Piedmont. The 7,490-acre Cheaha Wilderness Area is also part of the division. The 23-mile Talladega Scenic

Drive runs through the forest and follows the crest of Horse Black Mountain along SR 49 and SR 281. There are camping facilities, picnic areas, and nature programs. For more information, call (205) 926-9765 or 463-2272.

TUSKEGEE

Tuskegee National Forest, located in northeast Tuskegee off US Highway 80, consists of 11,000 acres of parkland. The Bartram National Recreation Trail offers an 8.5-mile tract of hiking trails. There are rolling hills and slow-moving streams between mountains and coastal plains, camping facilities, picnic areas and nature programs. For more information, call (334) 727-2652.

Army Corps of Engineers
Parks and Recreational Areas

CAMDEN

Clairborne Lake, located approximately 20 miles northwest of Monroeville, encompasses 5,930 acres of land. From Monroe go approximately 8 miles north on Highway 41, follow the signs on Monroe County Road 17 to Isaac Creek Parkway. There are campsites, picnic areas, hiking trails, a boat ramp so you can go boating, fishing, swimming and a visitors' center. For more information, call (334) 282-4254.

William "Bill" Dannelly Reservoir, go northwest of Camden on Highway 28 for 18 miles, then go north on Highway 5 to Alberta, then south on County Road 29 for approximately 9 miles and watch for the signs. The park encompasses 17,000 acres of land on the Alabama River. You will find camping, picnic areas, a boat ramp for boating, fishing and a visitors center. For more information, call (334) 573-2562.

DEMOPOLIS

Lake Demopolis, located off Black Warrior River, located 6 miles west of Demopolis on US Highway 80 to Lock and Dam Road. It encompasses 10,000 acres of parkland with camping facilities, picnic areas, hiking trails, a boat ramp for boating and fishing, and a visitors' center.

MONTGOMERY

R.E. "Bob" Woodruff Lake, located 25 miles west of Montgomery via US 80 to Robert F. Henry Lock and Dam Roads on the Alabama River, encompasses 12,510 acres. There are camping facilities, cabins, picnic areas, hiking trails, a boat ramp for boating and fishing and a visitors' center.

State Park and Recreational Area General Information

Division of Parks
Department of Conservation
and Natural Resources
64 North Union Street
Montgomery, AL 36130

(334) 242-3333
800-252-7275 – reservations

State Parks

ALEXANDER CITY

Wind Creek State Park, 7 miles southeast of Alexander City off Highway 63, is a 1,445-acre park offering camping facilities, a playground, picnic areas, boating, a boat ramp, fishing, swimming, hiking and bicycling trails and a nature program. For more information, call (205) 329-0845 or 800-ALA-PARK.

ANNISTON

Cheaha State Park, located 29 miles south of Anniston off SR 49 in the Talladega National Forest, encompasses 2,700 acres of parkland offering visitors camping facilities, picnic areas, hiking and bicycling trails, boating and fishing, swimming, nature programs and a visitors' center.

CHILDERSBURG

DeSoto Caverns Park, at 5181 DeSoto Parkway, 5 miles east of town, consists of 80 acres of parkland surrounded by onyx-marble caverns. The Creek Indians considered the caves a hallowed place. They believed that their forefathers had emerged from here to form the powerful Creek Nation. Tours of the Great Onyx Chamber and three Indian villages are available, plus picnic areas and camping facilities. For more information, call (205) 378-7252.

EUFAULA

Lakepoint Resort State Park, located 7 miles north of Eufaula, on Lake Eufaula, "bass capital of the world," off SR 431. This 1,220 acre park offers an 18-hole golf course, tennis courts, horse rentals, a playground, camping facilities, picnic areas, hiking and bicycling trails, boating, boat rentals, a full-service marina, fishing, swimming, nature programs and a visitors' center. For more information, call (334) 687-6676.

FOLEY

Gulf State Park Resort, located 10 miles south of Foley off SR 59, near Gulf Shores, is 6,150 acres of parkland on Pleasure Island. You will find 2.5 miles of pure white beaches and sand dunes. The park also has two freshwater lakes with canoeing and fishing, an 18-hole golf course, tennis courts, playground, as well as camping facilities, picnic areas, hiking and bicycle trails, boat rentals, fishing, swimming, nature programs, a visitors' center and an 825 foot pier. Deep-sea fishing is available through charter boat services. For more information, call 800-252-7275 or (334) 242-3260 or 981-8499.

FORT PAYNE

DeSoto State Park, located 8 miles northeast of Fort Payne along the Little River Canyon, off I-59. The park has the deepest canyons east of the Rocky Mountains. The scenery is breathtaking at this 16-mile-wide, 600 foot deep canyon. Be sure to visit DeSoto Falls, a breathtaking 100-foot drop, and Lookout Mountain Trail, a 20-mile scenic road that overlooks the west rim of the mountain. The trail begins at Route 89 at the Georgia state line, travels into Mentone, Alabama and continues to Dogtown and into Noccalula Falls at Gadsden. Visitors will find tennis courts, a playground, camping, hiking trails, picnic areas, fishing and swimming. For more information, call (205) 845-5380.

GUNTERSVILLE

Buck's Pocket State Park, in the northeastern part of the state, is 2,000 acres of hilly wooded land 2 miles north of Grove Oak. It has a mile-long trail leading into a 400-foot canyon. There is a playground, camping facilities, picnic areas, and boats to rent. For more information, call (205) 659-2000.

Lake Guntersville State Park, 6 miles northeast of Guntersville off SR 101, off the Tennessee River, is the 66,000-acre reservoir renowned for its largemouth and small mouth bass. The park offers boat rentals and a boat ramp, camping, picnic areas, hiking trails for you and your dog to explore, swimming, bicycle trails, nature programs and a visitors' center, as well as an 18-hole golf course, tennis courts and a playground. For more information, call 800-548-4553.

PELHAM

Oak Mountain State Park, located 15 miles south of Birmingham off I-65, exit 246, is a 10,000-acre park in the southernmost part of the Appalachian Mountain chain. The park has an 18-hole golf course, nature and hiking trails, a wonderful beach, a BMX bike track, tennis courts, horse, canoe and pedal boat rentals, rental cabins and campsites, picnic areas, a playground, boat ramps for boating, fishing, swimming, a visitors' center and nature programs. For more information, call (205) 620-2524 or 800-ALA-PARK.

ROGERSVILLE

Elk River at Joe Wheeler State Park is located 15 miles west of Athens off US Highway 72. From the red light in Rogersville go west approximately 1.5 miles to US Highway 72, Turn left at the park entrance. The lake is an offshoot of the Tennessee River between Wheeler Dam and Wheeler National Wildlife Refuge. Elk Lake offers visitors picnic areas, a boat ramp and rentals and fishing, plus 80 acres of land that you and your dog can explore. For more information, call (205) 247-5466.

SELMA

Paul M. Grist State Park, located 15 miles north of Selma off SR 22, encompasses 1,080 acres of parkland offering camping facilities, picnic areas, a playground area, hiking trails, and a boat ramp for boating and fishing.

TUSCALOOSA

Lake Lurleen State Park, located 12 miles northwest of Tuscaloosa off US Highway 82, encompasses 1,625 acres offering camping facilities, picnic areas, a playground, hiking trails, a boat ramp for boating and fishing, nature programs and a visitors' center.

WARRIOR

Rickwood Caverns State Park is located 5 miles north on I-65 between the Hayden Corner and Empire exits. Follow the signs to the entrance. The caverns are an interesting display of stalagmites and stalactites. There is a one-hour guided tour of the caverns; call for tour hours. You will find camping, swimming, hiking trails, picnic areas, a playground and horse rentals. For more information, call (205) 647-9692.

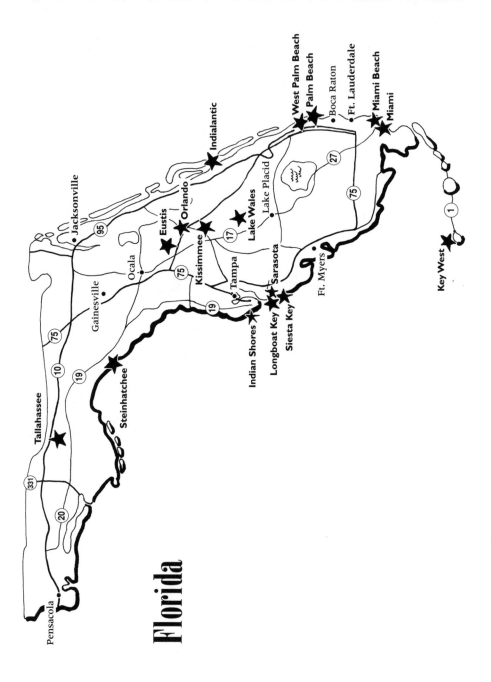

Florida

PETS WELCOME!

Florida

Dreamspinner Bed and Breakfast

Dreamspinner Bed and Breakfast
117 Diedrich Street
Eustis, FL 32726
888-479-1229 ▪ (352) 589-8082

Room Rates:	$105–$115, including full breakfast, afternoon English tea and evening wine and cheese.
Pet Charges or Deposits:	$25 per stay, $50 refundable deposit.
Rated: 4 Paws 🐾🐾🐾🐾	5 guest rooms with flowers, fresh fruit, bottled water, hot coffee and a newspaper delivered to your room.

A wraparound porch welcomes you to this charming bed and breakfast and its surrounding gardens with moss-laden oaks and romantically shaded benches and ponds. Antique roses, camellias and azaleas embellish over an acre of grounds. Elegant English fabrics adorn the well-appointed rooms. Art, antiques and fireplaces provide an eclectic, comfortable setting.

The historical integrity of the Dreamspinner has been maintained along with modern amenities for your comfort. The Victorian house, now called the Dreamspinner, was built in 1881. The kitchen and servants' quarters were originally separated from the main house by a breezeway, which now connects the two dwellings.

Your day will begin with a generous breakfast of homemade breads, jams and freshly brewed coffee. In the afternoon enjoy traditional English tea, followed later by wine and cheese each evening. Relax and enjoy the peace and tranquillity, or venture to nearby attractions such as Disney World, golf, tennis, antique shopping, fishing, horseback riding, or visit Ocala National Forest.

Oceanfront Cottages

Oceanfront Cottages
612 Wavecrest Avenue
Indialantic, FL 32903
800-785-8080 ▪ (407) 725-8474

Room Rates:	$89–$125
Pet Charges or Deposits:	$15 per day; up to $200 refundable deposit. Small pets only.
Rated: 3 Paws 🐾🐾🐾	4 suites with separate living and sleeping areas with king- or queen- sized beds, furnished with antiques, fully equipped kitchens, private patios with porch swings, oceanfront property, air conditioning, some fireplaces, in-room coffee, barbecue grills, laundry facilities, swimming pool and lush tropical garden, kayaks and bicycles.

A wake to the smell of the fresh ocean breeze and the sound of the gently rolling surf splashing on the shore from your suite at the Oceanfront Cottages. Located on the boardwalk overlooking the blue Atlantic Ocean, your accommodations will seem like your own private beach house.

Each suite is decorated with attractive antiques, including ball and clawfoot bathtubs, king- or queen-sized beds, a fully equipped kitchen, a spacious living room with a pullout sofa bed, and a remote-control color cable television with VCR. Each suite has a large, sliding glass door leading out to your own private patio with a Florida-style porch swing, wicker rockers and a barbecue grill, surrounded by tropical plants.

French doors lead to the pool, which is surrounded by a lush garden—a great place to relax and soak in the sun. The boardwalk overlooking the ocean is great for a stroll with your pooch. Bicycles are available to explore the shops and restaurants in town.

Casa Chica Cottages

Casa Chica Cottages
19000 Gulf Boulevard
Indian Shores, FL 33785
800-562-5335 ▪ (813) 596-1602

Room Rates:	$74–$84; weekly and monthly rates available.
Pet Charges or Deposits:	$15–$30 per stay. Small pets only.
Rated: 3 Paws 🐾🐾🐾	4 beach-front cottages, from studio to two-bedroom units with fully equipped kitchens, separate living and sleeping areas, color cable television, screened outdoor swim-spa pool, botanical gardens and a lovely private beach.

L ocated on the beach on the Gulf of Mexico is the Casa Chica Cottages. Your private, air-conditioned accommodations will include either a private studio, one- or two-bedroom cottage with tile floors, natural wood-paneled walls, comfortable beds, futon couches in the living area and a fully equipped kitchen.

The new swim-spa is a great place to unwind and is enclosed by a screened gazebo to keep insects away. The gently sloping, sandy white beach is perfect for a stroll with the dog, jogging, flying a kite, hunting for shells or just relaxing under a thatched umbrella with your favorite libation.

For the adventurous, the cottages are located less than forty minutes from downtown Tampa, less than two hours from Disney World and Epcot Center, and only minutes from shopping, golf courses, charter fishing boats, restaurants and other area attractions. Just be sure to return in time to watch the stunning sunset from your private beach-front cottage.

Center Court – Historic Inn and Cottages

Center Court – Historic Inn and Cottages
916 Center Street
Key West, FL 33040
800-797-8787 ▪ (305) 296-9292

Room Rates: $88–$298, including a deluxe continental breakfast.
Pet Charges or Deposits: $10. Manager's approval required.
Rated: 5 Paws 🐾🐾🐾🐾🐾 4 cottages and 10 suites with private bathrooms, some efficiency kitchens, televisions, ceiling fans, telephones, hair dryers, air-conditioning, heated pool, Jacuzzi, European-style sun deck, fish pond and exercise pavilion.

T rue to its name, Center Court is located on Center Street in one of Key West's oldest and most charming neighborhoods. Just half a block from the celebrated sights and sounds of Duval Street—many of the island's finest restaurants, art galleries and shops are neighbors here. Winner of two historical renovation awards for the buildings, the interiors have been decorated with original and unique local art. The same attention to detail and care have been given to landscaping. Lush tropical foliage laden with fruit and blooming with the vibrant colors of the Caribbean provide a year-round welcome.

Each of the accommodations at Center Court is as diverse as the cottages themselves. Every room is air-conditioned, with amenities generally reserved for resorts, such as a heated pool, relaxing Jacuzzi, European-style sun deck and exercise pavilion. All suites and cottages have private yards to accommodate your pet.

The Grand

The Grand
1116 Grinnell Street
Key West, FL 33040
888-947-2630 ▪ (305) 294-0590

Room Rates:	$38–$118
Pet Charges or Deposits:	$50 refundable deposit.
Rated: 3 Paws 🐾🐾🐾	6 non-smoking guest rooms and 4 suites with queen-sized beds, private entrances, efficiency kitchens and mini refrigerators, color cable television, swimming pool, outdoor showers, barbecue grills, laundry facilities and air conditioning.

L ocated in the historic section of Key West is The Grand. This tropical, historic inn was originally built as housing for Key West's burgeoning cigar industry in the late 1880s and has undergone many transformations over the years. The most recent was the restoration done in 1996 by the present owners.

The Grand was fully renovated with all the non-smoking guest rooms and suites offering private entrances, private baths, queen-sized beds, mini refrigerators, color televisions, air conditioning and some with efficiency kitchens. An outdoor barbecue area is available for guests to use and enjoy, as well as laundry facilities. The inn is located a short 5 blocks from the beach.

Whispers

Whispers
409 William Street
Key West, FL 33040
800-856-SHHH ▪ (305) 294-5969

Room Rates:	$75–$175, including gourmet breakfast.
Pet Charges or Deposits:	None.
Rated 4 Paws 🐾🐾🐾🐾	8 guest rooms with private bath, air conditioning, television and refrigerator, hot tub. Private beach and pool club included.

The house, listed on the National Register of Historic Places, sits on a sleepy, shaded street within view of the Gulf harbor, and is surrounded by a thirty-block historic district of distinctive 19th century buildings.

Today, ceiling fans whirl above rooms filled with antique furnishings, and congenial guests enjoy the cool porches and lush gardens at one of the island's most unique inns. A full membership at a nearby spa resort is included in your room rate, offering the use of a sauna, steam room, free weights, exercise equipment, pool and private beach.

A full and varied gourmet breakfast, such as lemon dill omelets, honey-maple ham and hot croissants topped with freshly sliced strawberries, is served daily throughout the year, and can be enjoyed either in the dining area or in the tropical gardens.

Summerfield Condo Resort

Summerfield Condo Resort
2425 Summerfield Way
Kissimmee, FL 34741
800-207-9582 ▪ (407) 847-7222

Room Rates:	$79–$149
Pet Charges or Deposits:	$25–$75 per stay. Manager's approval required.
Rated: 3 Paws 🐾🐾🐾	37 spacious condos, beautifully furnished with separate living and dining areas, remote-controlled cable television with VCR, telephone, fully equipped kitchens with full-size appliances, laundry facilities, swimming pool, playground, barbecue area and beautifully landscaped grounds.

I f you are looking for a vacation experience for the whole family, try the condominium-style accommodations of Summerfield Condo Resort. Each spacious townhouse is beautifully furnished and decorated with separate dining and living areas, complete with a sofa sleeper, 44-channel cable television with VCR and fully equipped kitchens and laundry facilities, including all of your detergents, soaps and paper goods supplied for you.

The resort is conveniently located within minutes of all Central Florida attractions, such as Disney World, Universal Studios and Sea World. Less than an hour away are Tampa's Busch Gardens, the Kennedy Space Center and many of the beautiful beaches of Florida's east and west coasts.

Chalet Suzanne
Country Inn and Restaurant

Chalet Suzanne Country Inn and Restaurant
3800 Chalet Suzanne Drive
Lake Wales, FL 33853-7060
800-433-6011 ▪ (941) 676-6011

Room Rates:	$139–$195, including a full breakfast. AAA discount.
Pet Charges or Deposits:	$20 per pet, plus deposit.
Rated: 4 Paws 😺😺😺😺	30 guest rooms, swimming pool, beautifully landscaped grounds with a lake, private airstrip, award-winning restaurant and cocktail lounge.

S urrounded by a 70-acre estate, the family-owned Chalet Suzanne Country Inn and Restaurant has been welcoming guests since 1931. This delightful inn of 30 rooms is a gracious oasis amid the excitement of Central Florida attractions.

Each room greets you with a different decor, through a private entrance by either courtyard or patio. Every corner of the inn glows with the charm of stained glass, antiques and old lamps from faraway places.

Chalet Suzanne has earned a glowing reputation for its cuisine. *Gourmet Magazine* called it "glorious." Meals are served in the unique setting of five quaint rooms located on several levels, overlooking the lake. The Soup Cannery is where the inn's delicious soups are processed and shipped all over the world. The soups have even been to the moon.

Riviera Beach Resort

Riviera Beach Resort
5451 Gulf of Mexico Drive
Longboat Key, FL 34228
(941) 383-2552

Room Rates:	$500–$985 per week
Pet Charges or Deposits:	$10 per day; $50 refundable deposit. Small dogs only. No cats, please. Manager's approval required.
Rated: 4 Paws	9 apartments with fully equipped kitchens, separate living areas, color television, air conditioning and heating, private patio, landscaped tropical gardens, private beach, shuffleboard court, barbecue grill, swimming, fishing and laundry facilities.

L ocated on its own private white sand beach in the Gulf of Mexico is the Riviera Beach Resort—one of the most secluded tropical beach settings on Longboat Key.

Spacious apartments overlook tropical gardens and calm blue waters, offering you a choice of one- or two-bedroom apartments with fully equipped kitchens. Each apartment offers the privacy of your own palm-shaded patio, complete with lounge chairs and barbecue.

Shops and gourmet restaurants beckon only a short walk away from the Riviera's tranquillity. Or stay on the beach and listen to the surf as you barbecue on the beach grill.

Amerisuites

Amerisuites
11520 Southwest 88th Street
Miami, FL 33176
(305) 279-8688

Room Rates:	$89–$129, including a continental buffet breakfast. AAA, AARP, AKC and ABA discounts.
Pet Charges or Deposits:	Call for deposits. Pets up to 20 lbs. Limit 2 pets per room.
Rated: 3 Paws 🐾🐾🐾	67 suites with refrigerators, microwaves, wet bars, coffee makers, in-room movies, separate living areas with sofa bed, laundry facilities, valet service, business center and heated swimming pool.

Amerisuites offers a wonderful alternative to your usual hotel accommodations. This affordable, all-suite hotel offers guests the luxury of a sleeping area with either king-sized or double beds, a separate living area with a full-size sofa bed and the added convenience of an in-room refrigerator, microwave, wet bar and coffee maker. All guests are invited to enjoy a complimentary deluxe continental buffet breakfast before heading out for a day of sightseeing or business meetings.

The hotel is located near shopping, the Metro Zoo, Coral Castle, Monkey Jungle, Parrot Jungle and Gardens, Florida International University, Everglades National Park and Miccosukee Indian Village and Gaming.

An outdoor heated swimming pool is surrounded by a large deck for sunbathing. The beautifully landscaped grounds are perfect for walking with your dog.

Club Hotel by DoubleTree

Club Hotel by DoubleTree
1101 N. W. 57th Avenue
Miami, FL 33126
888-444-CLUB ▪ (305) 266-0000

Room Rates:	$59–$135, including complimentary in-room breakfast. AAA, AARP, AKC and ABA discounts.
Pet Charges or Deposits:	$10 per day.
Rated: 3 Paws 🐾🐾🐾	264 guest rooms and 2 spacious suites with in-room movies, cable television, some with microwaves, refrigerators, VCRs, laundry facilities, self-service business center, jogging trails, pet exercise area, pool, restaurant and cocktail lounge.

When combining business with pleasure on your next trip to Miami, the Club Hotel by DoubleTree offers accommodations that are both business, and pet-friendly. Upon check-in you will receive the traditional DoubleTree greeting of two chocolate chip cookies.

Business travelers will appreciate the new "Club Room," a 7,000-square-foot multi-purpose work space allowing business travelers an office on the road. This 24-hour business center has quiet, private work spaces with a desk, bookshelves, electrical outlets, modem ports and a sliding door for privacy.

The Au Bon Pain Bakery Café is open from early morning to late at night with fresh baked food, made on the premises to serve you quickly. Menu selections include soups, salads, sandwiches, croissants, muffins and a variety of beverages.

Fontainebleau Hilton Resort and Towers

Fontainebleau Hilton Resort and Towers
4441 Collins Avenue
Miami Beach, FL 33140
800-548-8886 ▪ (305) 538-2000

Room Rates:	$149–$255, including continental breakfast.
Pet Charges or Deposits:	None.
Rated: 4 Paws 🐾🐾🐾🐾	1,206 guest rooms and 60 luxury suites, turndown service, in-room safe, iron and ironing board, beach access, saunas, steam rooms, whirlpools, 2 swimming pools (1 heated and 1 salt-water), health club, 7 lighted tennis courts, restaurants, coffee shops and cocktail lounge.

Set among twenty acres of lush tropical gardens overlooking the Atlantic Ocean on Miami Beach is the Fontainebleau Hilton Resort and Towers. The hotel offers recreational activities for guests of all ages. There are two magnificent outdoor pools—one is a freeform half-acre rock grotto with a cascading waterfall into a fresh water pool. There are also three whirlpool baths, seven lighted tennis courts, parasailing, paddle boats, hobie cats, boogie boards, hydro sleds, volleyball, basketball and two miles of beach. Spa facilities and state-of-the-art fitness and cardiovascular equipment are available as well.

The Fontainebleau Hilton offers award-winning dining and a wide variety of entertainment.

Ocean Front Hotel

Ocean Front Hotel
1230-38 Ocean Drive
Miami Beach, FL 33139
800-783-1725 ▪ (305) 672-2579

Room Rates:	$135–$475, including a continental breakfast.
Pet Charges or Deposits:	$15 per day. Manager's approval required.
Rated: 5 Paws 🐾🐾🐾🐾🐾	8 guest rooms and 21 luxury suites, many with ocean views and balconies, private in-room safe, color television, VCR, stereo with CD player, wet bar with refrigerator, central air conditioning, beach towels, bathrobes, rooms with private Jacuzzis, concierge service, restaurant and lounge.

Located in the heart of Miami Beach's world-renowned art deco district, just steps from the beautiful white sand beaches of the warm Atlantic Ocean is the exquisite Ocean Front Hotel.

The hotel's accommodations are delightfully decorated with a Mediterranean theme, complete with authentic furnishings from the 1930s. Each guest room offers a private in-room safe, color television, VCR, stereo with CD player, wet bar with refrigerator, soundproof windows, beach towels, bathrobes and central air conditioning. Many rooms have balconies with breathtaking ocean or courtyard views. For those choosing one of the penthouse suites, not only will you have wonderful ocean views from your private balcony, but the added bonus of a whirlpool tub and a private elevator.

While staying at the Ocean Front Hotel, be sure to sample some of the fine cuisine at the hotel's brasserie-style Les Deux Fontaines French Restaurant, which has a casual atmosphere and impeccable service.

Holiday Inn SunSpree Resort Lake Resort Buena Vista

Holiday Inn SunSpree Resort Lake Resort Buena Vista
13351 State Road 535
Orlando, FL 32821
800-366-6299 ▪ (407) 239-4500

Room Rates:	$99–$169 AAA and AARP discounts.
Pet Charges or Deposits:	None. Manager's approval required. Small pets only.
Rated: 3 Paws 🐾🐾🐾	371 guest rooms and 136 suites with mini kitchens, microwaves, refrigerators, coffee/tea makers, color cable television, VCR, hair dryers.

If you are looking for fun accommodations for the entire family, located within minutes of all the Central Florida attractions, the Holiday Inn SunSpree Resort Lake Resort Buena Vista is a wonderful choice. The spacious guest rooms are perfect for the busy family on vacation.

Your accommodations include amenities such as a mini kitchen with microwave, refrigerator, coffee and tea makers, color cable television with VCR, hair dryers and an in-room safe.

Both parents and children will love the family-friendly, themed Kid Suites: Castles, Forts, Tree Houses, Noah's Ark and more. In addition to the usual amenities, the Kid Suites have a separate sleeping area with bunk beds just for the kids, plus their own television with Super Nintendo, a cassette player and a play counter with chairs to keep them entertained.

Wellesley Inn

Wellesley Inn
5635 Windhover Drive
Orlando, FL 32819
800-444-8888 ▪ (407) 345-0026

Room Rates:	$40–$120, including a continental breakfast. AAA and AARP discounts.
Pet Charges or Deposits:	$10 per stay. Small pets only.
Rated: 3 Paws 🐾🐾🐾	94 guest rooms and 11 suites with in-room coffee maker, microwave, refrigerator, color cable television, heated pool, Jacuzzi, spas, health club, laundry facilities and data ports.

Located in Orlando, the world's top tourist destination, is the Wellesley Inn. This four-story, modern hotel offers guests the convenience of an in-room coffee maker, microwave, refrigerator and color cable television. A complimentary continental breakfast is included in your room rate.

If you are planning on visiting one of the many area attractions, such as Universal Studios, located only 1½ blocks from the hotel, Wet 'n Wild Water Park, Sea World, Disney World or Epcot Center, all located within a few minutes drive from the hotel, the front desk will gladly make arrangements for your tickets, with a discount price. The hotel features a health club, Jacuzzi and pool with sun deck.

Chesterfield Hotel

Chesterfield Hotel
363 Cocoanut Row
Palm Beach, FL 33480
800-243-7871 ▪ (561) 659-5800

Room Rates:	$89–$1099. AAA and AARP discounts.
Pet Charges or Deposits:	$150 refundable deposit. Dogs up to 40 lbs. No cats, please. Biscuits upon check-in; pet beds available.
Rated: 5 Paws ❀ ❀ ❀ ❀ ❀	43 guest rooms and 11 luxury suites, some refrigerators and safes, heated swimming pool, private cabaña, whirlpool, health club privileges, restaurant and cocktail lounge.

Located in the heart of Palm Beach, just off Worth Avenue, is the historic four-star Chesterfield Hotel. The elegant surroundings are an impressive blend of modern conveniences with the gracious standards of the Third Earl of Chesterfield, offering an uncompromised level of comfort and service.

The beautifully appointed accommodations have distinctive styles, specially chosen fabrics, elegant furnishings, deluxe marble bathrooms. Amenities include plush dressing robes, fine soaps, bottled mineral water and 24-hour room service.

The Chesterfield Hotel is located only three short blocks from the beach. The hotel's heated swimming pool, spa and private cabaña offer you a tropical setting in which to relax from dusk 'til dawn.

Heart of Palm Beach Hotel

Heart of Palm Beach Hotel
10 Royal Palm Way
Palm Beach, FL 33480
800-523-5377 ▪ (561) 655-5600

Room Rates:	$69–$219 AAA, AARP, AKC and ABA discounts. Packages available.
Pet Charges or Deposits:	Credit card as deposit. Manager approval required.
Rated: 4 Paws 🐾🐾🐾🐾	88 guest rooms and 2 suites with balcony or terrace, mini refrigerator, concierge service, limousine and bicycle rentals, underground parking, heated pool, restaurant and cocktail lounge.

A warm and friendly atmosphere welcomes you at the Heart of Palm Beach Hotel, a charming European-style hotel. Located in the heart of the island, on the ocean block of picturesque Royal Palm Way, you are only steps away from the beautiful blue Atlantic Ocean.

Your spacious accommodations will include such amenities as a refrigerator, color television and a balcony or terrace to enjoy the view. The pool is set in a delightful tropical setting, next to a garden pavilion.

There are world-famous Worth Avenue shops to keep you entertained, as well as the enchanting "Vias" dotted with boutiques and antique stores. The hotel is located within walking distance of many fine restaurants and area night life, or try the hotel's own Pleasant Peasant Restaurant and the Taps and Tapas Lounge, a popular spot to enjoy your favorite libation.

Banana Bay Club

Banana Bay Club
8254 Midnight Pass Road
Sarasota, FL 34242
888-6-BANBAY ▪ (941) 346-0113

Room Rates:	$90–$220; weekly and monthly rates available.
Pet Charges or Deposits:	$100 refundable deposit.
Rated: 4 Paws 🐾🐾🐾🐾	7 one- or two-bedroom apartments with fully equipped kitchens, all linens provided, remote control color cable television, air conditioning, ceiling fans, laundry facilities, barbecue grills, swimming pool, bikes and boats available.

If you are looking for a tropical getaway with swaying palm trees, flowering hibiscus and chirping birds, the Banana Bay Club offers all of that and more. This private paradise has five ground-floor guest rooms, fully furnished garden apartments, a studio apartment and a house overlooking the tranquil Heron Lagoon.

Everything is provided for you. Each unit has its own vibrant, Caribbean color scheme, is charmingly furnished, has a fully equipped kitchen, supplies all of your linens, beach chairs and its own private deck. There is also an inviting pool with relaxing spa jets, a canoe for exploring the lagoon, a rowboat for fishing and bicycles to explore the island.

Located a short distance from the resort is the world-famous white-sugar-sand beach, where sand sculpturing is an art, as well as the less crowded Turtle Beach. The aqua-colored waters of the Gulf are great for fishing, swimming and snorkeling.

The Beach Place

The Beach Place
5605 Avenida del Mare – Siesta Key
Sarasota, FL 34242
800-615-1745 ▪ (941) 346-1745

Room Rates:	$70–$125; weekly and monthly rates available. AAA, AARP, AKC and ABA discounts.
Pet Charges or Deposits:	$35 per stay
Rated: 3 Paws 🐾🐾🐾	4 one-bedroom housekeeping apartments with fully equipped kitchens, color cable television, VCR and movies, laundry facilities, bicycles, tennis and beach equipment, small library and outdoor heated pool in a tropical setting.

L ocated on one of the many islands fringing the Gulf Coast is The Beach Place. These cozy cottage apartments are set on one of the finest beaches in the world. Your apartment will accommodate up to four guests, and includes a fully equipped kitchen, a separate living room, a small library of books and a color cable television with VCR and movies.

The beach has been described as the finest in the world—two and a half miles of pure white sand that feels like talcum powder underfoot. You'll share your morning walks along the shoreline with sandpipers, pelicans and frigate birds. Out in the Gulf you may also see the local Sarasota dolphins as they cruise up and down along the coastline. And in the evenings there are the sunsets. Like the beach itself, these have been hailed as among the most spectacular in the world—awesome spectacles in blazing red and gold as the sun falls below the rim of the Gulf.

Beach Hideaway and Gulf Lookout

Beach Hideaway and Gulf Lookout
69 Avenue Massina
Siesta Key, FL 34242
800-452-2038 ▪ (941) 346-2326

Room Rates: $50–$80 AARP and AKC discounts.
Pet Charges or Deposits: $20 refundable deposit.
Rated: 3 Paws 🐾🐾🐾   20 suites on beach-front properties with fully equipped
                                       kitchens, linens, air conditioning, television with HBO,
                                       telephone by arrangement, Jacuzzi, hot tub, lounge chairs,
                                       laundry facilities and daily maid service available.

Located in a quiet, upscale, residential neighborhood, less than 125 steps from the sandbar-protected Gulf of Mexico, you will find Beach Hideaway and Gulf Lookout.

The one-, two- and three-bedroom suites, some with ocean views, have fully equipped kitchens, as well as daily maid service for an additional fee. Your pets will appreciate the large, spacious yards, as well as access to the beaches in front of the two properties.

Siesta Key is perfect for those who love water sports. Take a fishing cruise, rent a sailboat, snorkel, swim, water ski, explore the beautiful beaches or take a romantic dinner cruise. For land lovers, there are excellent golf courses, tennis courts, wonderful shops, restaurants, antique shops, galleries and museums. Once you have explored all that the Keys have to offer, return to the comforts of your own private beach retreat.

Turtle Beach Resort

Turtle Beach Resort
9049 Midnight Pass Road
Siesta Key, FL 34231
(941) 349-4554

Room Rates:	$120–$280; weekly rates and packages available. AAA discount.
Pet Charges or Deposits:	10% of room rate; deposit on large dogs only. Manager's approval required.
Rated: 4 Paws 🐾🐾🐾🐾	2 guest rooms and 3 suites with fully equipped kitchens with microwaves and coffee makers, honor bars, private hot tubs and patios, laundry facilities, daily maid service available, paddle boats, fishing rods, beach chairs, bicycles, gazebo, room service and docking facilities.

Turtle Beach Resort is a small, Key West-style resort located on the south end of the island, where the large sea turtles nest. There are spectacular views of the Gulf of Mexico and room to dock your boat. You can fish off the pier, go paddle boating, bike along the shoreline, or head into Siesta Village to browse through shops. For those seeking solitude with a good book, a hammock and warm breeze await.

Guest villas are one or two bedrooms. All are equipped with a kitchen area, an enclosed private patio with outdoor spa and a barbecue grill. The larger units have a living and dining room. Lush landscape surrounds you while you enjoy a swim in the outdoor heated pool. Banana trees, giant elephant ear and red hibiscus plants grow unchecked in the warm climate.

Steinhatchee Landing Resort and Inn

Steinhatchee Landing Resort and Inn
Highway 51, North – PO Box 789
Steinhatchee, FL 32359
800-584-1709 ▪ (352) 498-3513

Room Rates:	$50–$280; weekly and monthly rates available. AAA, AARP, AKC and ABA discounts.
Pet Charges or Deposits:	$250 refundable deposit.
Rated: 4 Paws 🐾🐾🐾🐾	17 spacious suites, many with fully equipped kitchens and separate living areas; 20 Victorian-style cottages with fully equipped kitchens, fireplaces, spas, whirlpool baths, health club, river views and private docks, in a wooded setting on or near the river.

The Steinhatchee area has been a favorite destination for those who enjoy the beauty of the great outdoors. Some of the best fresh water and saltwater fishing in the nation takes place here. Great care has been taken to preserve the rustic beauty of this wooded river setting. There are gazebos and footbridges scattered throughout, providing guests with peaceful places to relax in tranquil surroundings.

The Steinhatchee Landing Resort and Inn offers the choice of a spacious suite or a private Victorian cottage, set amongst the beautiful Spanish-moss-draped oak trees.

Hundreds of miles of old wooded Indian trails are here for you to hike or bicycle, and there is swimming, horseback riding and bird watching.

La Quinta Inn

La Quinta Inn
2905 North Monroe Street
Tallahassee, FL 32303
800-531-5900 ▪ (904) 385-7172

Room Rates:	$62–$102, including a continental breakfast. AAA and AARP discounts.
Pet Charges or Deposits:	None.
Rated: 3 Paws 🐾🐾🐾	152 spacious rooms and 2 suites with in-room coffee makers, color television and entertainment system, microwave, refrigerator, valet laundry, swimming pool, data ports.

Whether traveling on business, looking for a weekend getaway or on a family vacation, the La Quinta Inn offers guests spacious rooms with all the amenities. From the fresh decor to the separate sleeping and living areas, and the in-room microwaves and refrigerators, you will feel right at home in your quiet accommodations. Kids of all ages will enjoy the latest video games and the in-room first-run movies viewed on the expanded entertainment system.

Included in the price of your room is the complimentary First Light breakfast, featuring your choice of cereal, fresh fruit, bagels, pastries, juice, milk and coffee. For those who wish to work off their breakfast, the large swimming pool is great for a few laps or a relaxing swim. Both you and your dog will appreciate the beautifully landscaped grounds and the lovely courtyard, perfect for a morning stroll.

The Royal Palm House Bed and Breakfast

The Royal Palm House Bed and Breakfast
3215 Spruce Avenue
West Palm Beach, FL 33407
800-NU-ROOMS ▪ (561) 863-9863

Room Rates:	$75–$150, including a continental breakfast.
Pet Charges or Deposits:	$5 per day; $25 refundable deposit. Small pets only. Manager's approval required.
Rated: 3 Paws 🐾🐾🐾	3 guest rooms and 3 suites with private baths, air conditioning, spacious grounds with freeform pool,

The Royal Palm House Bed and Breakfast was built in 1925, during the West Palm Beach land boom. This tropical Dutch Colonial-style home features single guest rooms and suites with private baths.

Each room has its own unique style of furnishing and atmosphere. The spacious grounds are planted with lush tropical vegetation which surrounds the lovely freeform swimming pool. It is a great place to relax and sun bathe.

The West Palm Beach area is located on Florida's "Gold Coast," named for the gold salvaged from shipwrecks off the coast. Besides having some of the most beautiful beaches in the world, there are numerous theaters and playhouses, Worth Avenue for shopping, plus numerous golf courses, tennis courts, croquet clubs and polo fields here.

Florida

Please Note: *Pets must be on a leash at all times and may be restricted to certain areas. For directions, use fees, pet charges and general information, contact the numbers listed below.*

Florida State Parks General Information

Department of Environmental Protection
Division of Recreation and Parks
Marjory Stoneman Douglas Bldg.
3900 Commonwealth Blvd.
Mail Station 535
Tallahassee, FL 32399
(904) 487-1462

State Parks

BUNNELL

Bulow Plantation Ruins State Park, 9 miles southeast of Bunnell on CR 2001 (Old Kings Road), consists of 109 historic acres of parkland, offering canoeing, picnicking, nature trails, a ramp for boating and fishing. For information, call (904) 517-2084.

BUSHNELL

Withlacoochee State Park, located in Central Florida west of Bushnell, consists of 113,000 acres with hunting, camping, horse rental, picnicking, nature trails, a ramp for boating, fishing and swimming.

FORT PIERCE

Fort Pierce State Park, located 3 miles east of Fort Pierce on SR A1A, has 340 historic acres with picnicking, nature and biking trails, boating, fishing, swimming and scuba diving and skin diving.

HOLLYWOOD

Topeekeegee Yugnee State Park, located a half mile west of I-95 on Sheridan Street (SR 822) in Hollywood, consists of 150 acres with miniature golf, a water slide, camping, picnicking, nature and biking trails, paddleboat rentals, fishing and swimming. For more information, call the Greater Hollywood Chamber of Commerce (954) 923-4000.

ST. GEORGE ISLAND

St. George Island State Park, located off US 98 via CRs G1A and 300 on St. George Island, consists of 1,833 acres offers bird watching, camping, picnicking, nature trails, boating, boat rentals, fishing and swimming.

ST. PETERSBURG

Maximo State Park, at 34th St. and Pinellas Point Dr. S., consists of 65 acres with an observation tower, playground, picnic areas, nature and biking trails, a ramp for boating and fishing. For more information, call the St. Petersburg Area Visitors Bureau at (800) 683-1000 or (941) 922-3575.

SUN CITY

Little Manatee River State Park, located 4 miles south of Sun City off US 301, consists of 1,634 acres offers visitors horse rentals, camping, picnicking, nature trails and a boat ramp.

TALLAHASSEE

Lake Talquin State Park, located 20 miles west of Tallahassee off SR 20 on Vause Road, consists of 30,000 acres with picnic areas, nature trails and fishing.

Other Recreational Areas

COCONUT CREEK

Tradewinds Recreation Area, at 3066 Sample Road in Coconut Creek, consists of 90 acres with a museum, botanical gardens, horse rentals, pony and hay rides, picnicking, nature and bike trails, boat rental, and fishing. For more information, call the Coconut Creek Chamber of Commerce at (954) 977-4400.

DAVIE

Tree Tops Recreation Area, at 3900 S.W. 100th Ave. in Davie, consists of 256 acres. It has horse rentals, picnicking, nature trails, boat rentals, fishing and a visitors' center. For more information, call the Fort Lauderdale Parks and Recreation hotline at (954) 761-5363 or the Visitor's Bureau (800) 356-1662 or (954) 765-4466.

Georgia

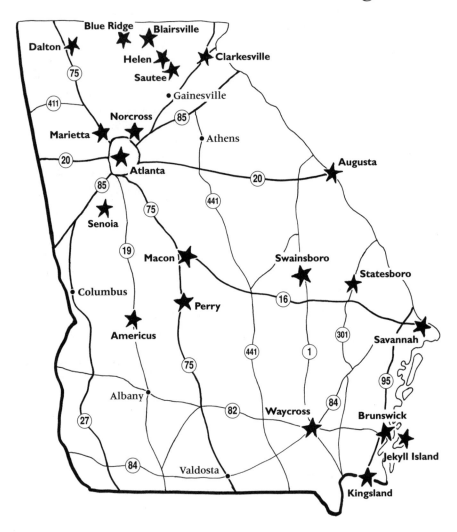

PETS WELCOME!

Georgia

The Pathway Inn Bed and Breakfast

The Pathway Inn Bed and Breakfast
501 South Lee Street
Americus, GA 31709
800-889-1466 ▪ (912) 928-2078

Room Rates:	$65–$137; including full breakfast. AAA, AARP, AKC and ABA discounts.
Pet Charges or Deposits:	$5 per day. Manager's approval required. Small dogs only.
Rated: 4 Paws 🐾🐾🐾🐾	5 guest rooms with private baths, some with whirlpools, king- or queen-sized beds with down comforters, fireplaces, ceiling fans, televisions and telephones.

When looking for an upscale bed and breakfast inn offering personal attention and pampering, visit The Pathway Inn Bed and Breakfast. Here guests will find attractive, individually decorated rooms with king- or queen-sized beds, luxurious down comforters, fireplaces and private bathrooms with whirlpool tubs.

Make sure to tear yourself away from your room long enough to enjoy the sumptuous candlelit breakfast served each morning, and the complimentary refreshments, wine and assorted beverages served in the evening. You will want to experience the true Southern hospitality of this gracious small town, too. There are plenty of historical sights and lots of antique shops to explore in nearby Andersonville, a Civil War town. Dog-sitting is available if needed.

Bed and Breakfast Atlanta

Bed and Breakfast Atlanta
1801 Piedmont Avenue, NE, Suite 208
Atlanta, GA 30324
(404) 875-0525

Room Rates:	$55–$150, most include breakfast.
Pet Charges or Deposits:	Call for charges and deposits.
Rated: 4 Paws 🐾🐾🐾🐾	80 bed and breakfast inns, homestays and cottages, with an assortment of amenities ranging from budget to luxury accommodations.

Bed and Breakfast Atlanta is a professional reservation service, providing visitors to the Atlanta area with lodging in carefully inspected and selected inns, homestays and guest cottages. Most accommodations are centrally located in desirable neighborhoods and suburban communities, offering a variety of amenities to please every traveler.

Each accommodation is unique and reflects the style and tastes of Atlanta. You are assured that each accommodation meets the standards of comfort, cleanliness and hospitality you seek. The service will make sure that your pet is welcome, too.

Beverly Hills Inn

Beverly Hills Inn
65 Sheridan Drive, NE
Atlanta, GA 30305
800-331-8520 ▪ (404) 233-8520

Room Rates:	$90–$160, including continental breakfast.
Pet Charges or Deposits:	$10 per stay. Small pets only. Pets must be in carrier when guest is not in the room.
Rated: 3 Paws 🐾🐾🐾	18 charming European-style suites, all with private baths and kitchens, sitting area with complimentary wine, furnished with antiques, set in a residential neighborhood.

L ocated in the prestigious Buckhead residential area, minutes from downtown Atlanta, is the European-style Beverly Hills Inn. Your accommodations reflect a way of life seldom encountered in today's world; one filled with the charm of the past and the conveniences of the present.

Each of the delightful, airy suites is furnished with period antiques and Oriental rugs. Relax in the sitting area with your complimentary wine or step out onto your private balcony which is scented with the fragrance of fresh seasonal flowers. Guests are invited to browse the inn's library and select a good book or magazine to curl up with during leisure hours. The Beverly Hills Inn also provides the modern conveniences of a fax, computer and a copying machine.

A leisurely continental breakfast with seasonal fresh fruits and pastries is served each morning. There are plenty of places for you and your dog to enjoy a brisk walk in this lovely residential neighborhood.

The Georgian Terrace

The Georgian Terrace
659 Peachtree Street
Atlanta, GA 30308
800-651-2316 ▪ (404) 897-1991

Room Rates:	$140–$175
Pet Charges or Deposits:	None. Limit 2 pets per room.
Rated: 5 Paws 🐾🐾🐾🐾🐾	320 suites with microwaves, honor bars, fully equipped kitchens, roof-top swimming pool, fitness center.

Since 1911, The Georgian Terrace—with its Southern-style Parisian architecture—has been one of Atlanta's grand hotels, reflecting the grandeur and opulence of a bygone era. Listed on the National Register of Historic Places, the hotel has recently been lovingly restored to its original magnificence while maintaining modern amenities expected in an upscale hotel.

To maintain the historical feel of the hotel, a palette of rich, warm, neutral colors and subtle textures, fine mahogany furniture, specially woven draperies and fine art have been incorporated into the decor of the one-, two- or three-bedroom suites. The Georgian Terrace Health Club features a state-of-the-art exercise room and a fabulous roof-top junior Olympic swimming pool. For the four-legged guests, the concierge will give you directions to favorite neighborhood parks and even arrange for doggie day care if needed.

Homewood Suites Hotel

Homewood Suites Hotel
3200 Cobb Parkway
Atlanta, GA 30339
800-CALL-HOME ▪ (770) 988-9449

Room Rates:	$109–$169, including continental breakfast and an evening social.
Pet Charges or Deposits:	$75 nonrefundable deposit. Manager's approval required.
Rated: 4 Paws 😺😺😺😺	124 spacious one- and two-bedroom suites with separate living areas, some with fireplaces, kitchens, televisions with VCRs, pool and Jacuzzi, fitness center, convenience shop and laundry facilities.

When looking for a home away from home for a short business trip or an extended family vacation, the Homewood Suites Hotel is a natural choice. Here guests will find spacious, one- or two-bedroom suites with separate living and sleeping areas. Some include inviting fireplaces where you can relax with a good book or a glass of wine. The fully equipped kitchens are perfect for preparing your own meals or for a quick, late-night snack.

Start your day off with the complimentary continental breakfast buffet before heading out for a day of meetings or sightseeing. For those with a leisurely day planned, you may wish to relax by the pool, swim a few laps, work out in the hotel's fitness center, soak in the outdoor Jacuzzi or take your dog for a walk on the spacious grounds.

Radisson Suites Inn

Radisson Suites Inn
3038 Washington Road
Augusta, GA 30907
800-333-3333 ▪ (706) 868-1800

Room Rates:	$59–$99, including full breakfast and evening cocktails. AAA and AARP discounts.
Pet Charges or Deposits:	$25 per stay.
Rated: 3 Paws ❖❖❖	176 luxury suites with separate living area, refrigerator, microwave, coffee maker, 2 televisions, 3 telephones, outdoor pool, landscaped courtyard, health club passes, restaurant and lounge.

Located in the heart of the business and entertainment district, the Radisson Suites offers handsomely furnished, comfortable and spacious guest rooms. The Jacuzzi Suites and Ambassador Suites come with a separate living room, a kitchenette with microwave oven, refrigerator, coffee maker and all the amenities of home.

Start your day off with the complimentary breakfast buffet before heading out to explore the area attractions, such as the award-winning revitalized Augusta Riverfront (located along the Savannah River), the National Register of Historic Places, the Morris Museum of Art or the National Golf Club.

Both you and your dog will enjoy a stroll through the attractive landscaped courtyard. In the evening, the inn's restaurant offers casual dining with a varied menu. Don't forget the complimentary evening cocktails.

7 Creeks Housekeeping Cabins

7 Creeks Housekeeping Cabins
5109 Horseshoe Cove Road
Blairsville, GA 30512
(706) 745-4753

Room Rates:	$60–$90
Pet Charges or Deposits:	None. Manager's approval required.
Rated: 3 Paws ❀❀❀	6 cabins offering one, two and three bedrooms, all with fireplaces, televisions, covered porches, full kitchens, laundry facilities, private lake, barbecue grills and picnic tables.

L ocated near Brasstown Bald, Georgia's highest mountain, and one of the South's most beautiful areas, is 7 Creeks Housekeeping Cabins. These comfortable cabins provide guests with everything you'll need, except linens and food. The cabins are set in the middle of 70 acres of mountainous terrain, offering a tranquil setting with breathtaking views from your private covered porch.

A crystal-clear lake is stocked for fishing. Guests may fish (no license required), spend the day relaxing on the lake or picnicking in the covered pavilion. Rental boats are available. You may also want to take a moment to visit the goats and other farm animals on the property, as well as the resident dog.

Misty Mountain Inn and Cottages

Misty Mountain Inn and Cottages
4376 Misty Mountain Lane
Blairsville, GA 30512
888-MISTY MN ▪ (706) 745-4786

Room Rates:	$50–$85, including a continental breakfast for bed and breakfast guests.
Pet Charges or Deposits:	$25 per stay; $25 refundable deposit. Proof of inoculations and manager's approval required.
Rated: 4 Paws 🐾🐾🐾🐾	4 bed and breakfast rooms with private baths, fireplaces, furnished with antiques and queen-sized beds; plus 6 private cottages, each with a full bath, fireplace, private porch and fully equipped kitchen.

Misty Mountain Inn and Cottages offers guests their choice of four bed and breakfast accommodations with private baths and whirlpool tubs, comfortable queen-sized beds, charming antique furnishings, private balconies and a complimentary continental breakfast for bed and breakfast guests.

For those traveling with their pets, there are six private cottages, all with fully equipped eat-in kitchens, wood-burning fireplaces and queen-sized beds. The private porches are perfect for grilling your dinner on the supplied hibachi, as you watch the sun go down.

There are three ponds and a picnic area for your enjoyment before you venture out into the neighboring areas for a day at one of the many lakes along the Appalachian Trail.

Blue Ridge Mountain Cabins, Inc.

Blue Ridge Mountain Cabins
P.O. Box 1102
Blue Ridge, GA 30513
(706) 632-8999

Room Rates:	$75–$100 per day; weekly rates available.
Pet Charges or Deposits:	$20 per pet per stay. Pets up to 35 lbs.
Rated: 3 Paws 🐾🐾🐾	36 furnished cabins located on the mountainside, near a lake, stream, creek, river, or set in the woods; with fully equipped kitchens, grills, large porches, fireplaces with wood supplied, linens, heat and air conditioning, laundry facilities, dishwasher, microwave, telephone, TV, VCR and some dog runs.

Escape to the beautiful north Georgia mountains and relax on the front porch of one of the Blue Ridge Mountain Cabins. These completely furnished cabins have fully equipped kitchens and supplies you need for a weekend getaway or a relaxing vacation. All you need to bring is your food and your spirit of adventure. The cabins are located either on the mountainside or set in the woods, all with beautiful views, near a lake, stream, creek or river.

There are plenty of places to enjoy tubing or white-water rafting on the Toccoa or Ocoee rivers, or go swimming, boating or fishing on Lake Blue Ridge. You and your pet can commune with nature while enjoying a picnic in the Chattahoochee National Forest. The cabins are all centrally located near shops, grocery stores, restaurants and recreational areas to keep you entertained and well-fed.

Comfort Inn

Comfort Inn
5308 New Jesup Highway
Brunswick, GA 31523
800-551-7591 ▪ (912) 264-6540

Room Rates:	$59–$89, including continental breakfast. AAA, AARP, AKC and ABA discounts.
Pet Charges or Deposits:	None
Rated: 3 Paws 🐾🐾🐾	118 guest rooms, cable television, some with microwaves, refrigerators, coffee makers, valet laundry service, swimming pool and 24-hour restaurant.

Brunswick's Comfort Inn is conveniently located only minutes from area casinos at St. Simons, Sea Island, Jekyll Island, Sapelo Island and Cumberland Island. Guests will find spacious, smoking or nonsmoking rooms featuring card-key locks with interior entrances and remote-control cable television. A deluxe all-you-can-eat continental breakfast featuring fresh fruits, hot and cold cereal, toast, pastries, bagels and juices is included in your room rate.

The Comfort Inn boasts the area's largest outdoor swimming pool, surrounded by attractive landscaped grounds. Attractions very near the inn are the Emerald Princess Cruise and Casino ship and several golf courses, with packages available.

Embassy Suites – Golden Isles

Embassy Suites – Golden Isles
500 Mall Boulevard
Brunswick, GA 31520
800-432-3229 ▪ (912) 264-6100

Room Rates:	$69–$99, including full breakfast and evening cocktails and beverages. AAA discounts.
Pet Charges or Deposits:	$10 per day.
Rated: 4 Paws 🐾🐾🐾🐾	130 luxury suites with coffee makers, microwaves, refrigerators, cable television, whirlpools, swimming pool, exercise room, valet laundry and café.

L ocated only minutes from the scenic Colonial Coast, next to Glynn Place Mall, is the Embassy Suites – Golden Isles. Here you will find large suites with private bedrooms, separate living areas, with the added convenience of in-room microwaves, refrigerators and coffee makers.

A complimentary breakfast of fresh-baked breads, pastries, eggs, bacon, sausage, French toast, home fries, Georgia grits and hot coffee or tea is served daily. The Embassy Suites offers a fitness center and outdoor pool.

Local attractions and sightseeing include Jekyll Island, a day at the beautiful beaches of St. Simons or aquatic thrills at one of the local water parks.

Habersham Hollow Country Cabins

Habersham Hollow Country Cabins
254 Habersham Hollow Lane
Clarkesville, GA 30523
(706) 754-5147

Room Rates:	$65 and up. Weekly rates available.
Pet Charges or Deposits:	Call for charges and deposit. Manager's approval required.
Rated: 3 Paws 🐾🐾🐾	2 furnished cabins with complete kitchens, microwaves, air conditioning, wood-burning fireplace, television and private decks with barbecue grills.

Nestled in the northeast Georgia mountains, the Habersham Hollow Country Cabins offer guests a peaceful, wooded oasis of serenity and solitude. Fully furnished cabins include linens, complete kitchens, wood-burning fireplaces and a private deck to relax while grilling your freshly caught fish. With no telephones to distract you, it's a wonderful location to really get away from it all.

Centrally located near town, you have several restaurants and antique shops to choose from. You are only a short drive from recreational areas, where you can spend the day hiking, swim in a river, go tubing, canoeing, horseback riding or fishing in one of the many lakes and streams.

Holiday Inn

Holiday Inn
515 Holiday Drive
Dalton, GA 30720
(706) 278-0500

Room Rates:	$75. AAA and AARP discounts.
Pet Charges or Deposits:	None
Rated: 3 Paws 🐾🐾🐾	199 guest rooms, coffee makers, cable television, swimming pool, fitness facilities, laundry facilities, room service, restaurant and cocktail lounge.

Dalton's Holiday Inn is central to Nashville, Knoxville, Chattanooga and Atlanta. Set in a convenient downtown location, you are only blocks from Dalton College and within minutes of area attractions, such as Lookout Mountain, Rock City, the Tennessee Aquarium, the Chickamauga Battlefield Park and Museum and the Incline Railroad.

Your accommodations include a spacious room with a king-sized bed or two double beds, in-room coffee makers and remote-control cable television and movies. The inn also offers a fitness facility and pool. There are great walking paths where you and your dog can stretch your legs.

Sensations Restaurant features daily luncheon buffets during the week, seafood buffets on Friday evenings, a prime rib buffet on Saturday evenings and Sunday brunch. Room service is available for those who wish to take advantage of in-room dining.

The Helendorf River Inn and Towers

The Helendorf River Inn and Towers
33 Munichstrasse
Helen, GA 30545
800-445-2271 ▪ (706) 878-2271

Room Rates:	$44–$160
Pet Charges or Deposits:	$10 per day. Manager's approval required.
Rated: 3 Paws 🐾🐾🐾	90 tower and river rooms, 7 spacious suites, some rooms with kitchenettes, sitting rooms, fireplaces, in-room Jacuzzis, riverfront balconies and enclosed, heated pool.

S et on the banks of the crystal-clear Chattahoochee River in the city of Helen, northern Georgia's Alpine village, is the charming Helendorf River Inn and Towers. All the rooms have color cable TV, telephones, individual heat and air conditioning. The spacious river rooms and beautifully decorated suites are extra large, offering romantic fireplaces with slate hearths, Jacuzzis, a complete kitchen and your own private balcony overlooking the rushing waters.

The area is popular for festivals, hot-air ballooning, sports events and seasonal scenery. The inn's location is convenient to canoeing, tubing, fishing, swimming, enjoying a leisurely day of picnicking along the banks of the Chattahoochee River or taking a walk with your dog on the laurel-covered hillsides.

Clarion Resort Buccaneer

Clarion Resort Buccaneer
85 Beachview Drive
Jekyll Island, GA 31527
800-253-5955 ▪ (912) 635-2261

Room Rates:	$79–$159. AAA, AARP, AKC and ABA discounts.
Pet Charges or Deposits:	None
Rated: 4 Paws 🐾🐾🐾🐾	205 oceanside guest rooms with private balconies or patios, most with ocean views, free movies, coffee makers, efficiency kitchens, spacious grounds, beach, pool, whirlpool, tennis court, playground, shuffleboard, area transportation.

Nestled in the tree-covered dunes of Georgia's beautiful Jekyll Island is the Clarion Resort Buccaneer. This resort offers guests a beautiful setting, combined with a leisurely atmosphere and all the amenities of a fine Colonial Coast resort. Once a private winter retreat for America's wealthiest families, Jekyll Island is now enjoyed by all. The spacious guest rooms, efficiency kitchens, large executive rooms and plush suites are richly appointed, featuring sumptuous fabrics, lush carpets and large bathrooms.

Guests may relax by the pool, soak in the hot tub, enjoy a friendly game of cards in the game room, play tennis, bike on the miles of paths, take a romp with their dog along the 10-mile beachfront or take a walk through the sprawling canopy of oak trees. Also located on the island are golf courses, a major tennis complex, boating, fishing, biking, shopping and Summer Waves water park. There are also guided tours of the historical homes that grace the island.

Comfort Inn Island Suites

Comfort Inn Island Suites
711 Beachview Drive
Jekyll Island, GA 31527
800-204-0202 ▪ (912) 635-2211

Room Rates:	$59–$189, including continental breakfast. AAA, AARP, AKC and ABA discounts.
Pet Charges or Deposits:	None
Rated: 3 Paws 🐾🐾🐾	178 rooms with oceanfront views, whirlpool, private patio or balcony, pool, playground, outdoor hot tubs, in-room movies.

Enjoy the natural beauty, abundant wildlife and recreation of Jekyll Island from your own spacious, oceanfront room at the Comfort Inn Island Suites. Guests are pampered with a complimentary continental breakfast each morning.

The Lanai Suites are deluxe oceanfront rooms, each with a private whirlpool, overlooking the Atlantic, exquisitely furnished with queen or double beds and private balcony or patio. The Ocean Suites offer a kitchenette, extra-large oceanfront accommodations with two double beds and a separate living area, private patio or balcony.

Jekyll Island offers a mild, year-round climate, perfect for sailing, golfing or strolling the beach with your dog. Relax in the sun on the poolside deck which boasts an outdoor dining area, lush greenery, a playground, outdoor hot tubs and beautiful beachfront. Tour the historical millionaires' homes or explore the island on 20 miles of jogging and bike trails.

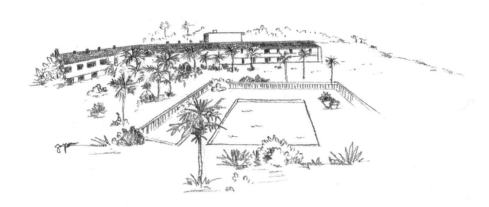

Villas by the Sea

Villas by the Sea
1175 North Beachview Drive
Jekyll Island, GA 31527
800-841-6262 ▪ (912) 635-2521

Room Rates: $84–$239. Weekly rates available.
Pet Charges or Deposits: $50–$100 per stay. No deposit.
Rated: 4 Paws 🐾🐾🐾🐾 168 condominium, oceanfront villas offering one to three bedrooms with fully equipped kitchens, full maid service, televisions, balconies, laundry facilities, baby-sitting services, 18-hole golf course, tennis, restaurant and cocktail lounge.

Nestled among 17 acres of windswept oaks and lush natural landscaping, Villas by the Sea offers one-, two- and three-bedroom villas, many of which overlook 2,000 feet of beautiful white sand beach. Each unit comes complete with a fully equipped kitchen, separate living and dining areas with private balconies or decks offering breathtaking views of the island or the sea. Each villa is individually owned and attractively decorated to make you feel right at home, with the added bonus of optional maid service.

Experience the Island's famed amenities, such as 63 holes of championship golf, lighted indoor-outdoor tennis, cable water skiing and the celebrated Historic District. You'll also enjoy a fishing pier, fishing charters, 14 miles of scenic bike paths, a Nautilus-equipped fitness center and a water park.

Holiday Inn

Holiday Inn
Interstate 95 and Highway 40
Kingsland, GA 31548
800-322-6866 ▪ (912) 729-3000

Room Rates:	$59–$189. AAA, AARP, AKC and ABA discounts.
Pet Charges or Deposits:	None
Rated: 3 Paws 🐾🐾🐾	156 guest rooms with individual climate control, cable television and in-room movies, coffee makers, some rooms with kitchens and refrigerators; swimming and wading pools, whirlpool, laundry facilities, restaurant and cocktail lounge.

At the Kingsland Holiday Inn you will find Southern hospitality at a conveniently located establishment. The elegant guest rooms offer a relaxing atmosphere with individual climate control, cable television and in-room movies and coffee makers. Kitchenettes and non-smoking rooms are also available.

The expansive courtyards offer a feeling of privacy, the perfect place for you and your dog to take a stroll. The fenced swimming area is great for the whole family. The children will enjoy having a wading pool just their size while the parents relax on the expansive deck or swim in the main pool.

There are several popular area attractions nearby, such as the Okefenokee Wildlife Refuge, Cumberland Island and Fernandina Beach.

The Plantation Restaurant offers down-home cooking and coastal favorites. The inn's authentic country store is delightful and has a variety of unusual gifts and country collectibles. Tootie's Nightclub is the place to enjoy your favorite libation, dancing and live entertainment.

Holiday Inn and Conference Center

Holiday Inn and Conference Center
3590 Riverside Drive
Macon, GA 31210
888-394-8552 ▪ (912) 474-2610

Room Rates:	$68–$74, including breakfast buffet. AAA, AARP, AKC and ABA discounts.
Pet Charges or Deposits:	None. Small pets only.
Rated: 3 Paws 🐾🐾🐾	200 guest rooms with in-room coffee, remote-control televisions, hair dryers, microwaves, refrigerators, turn-down service, outdoor pool, 24-hour exercise room, jogging trails, restaurant and cocktail lounge.

Conveniently located on I-75 at Arkwright Road and Riverside Drive, the centrally located Holiday Inn has set the standard for continual innovative service and amenities that provide the best value for your money.

The well-appointed guest rooms offer you in-room coffee makers, hair dryers, microwaves, refrigerators, a 24-hour exercise room, jogging trails and a beautiful outdoor swimming pool. Business travelers will appreciate the extra business services available.

Tradition's Restaurant located at the Holiday Inn features continental cuisine served in casual elegance. Enjoy an after-dinner drink at Chasen's Lounge, Macon's favorite night spot, featuring a live DJ.

Drury Inn – Atlanta Northwest

Drury Inn – Atlanta Northwest
1170 Powers Ferry Place
Marietta, GA 30067
800-DRURY-INN ▪ (770) 612-0900

Room Rates:	$69–$89, including buffet breakfast and evening beverage reception. AAA and AARP discounts.
Pet Charges or Deposits:	None. Manager's approval required. Small pets only.
Rated: 3 Paws 🐾🐾🐾	143 guest rooms and 23 luxury suites, king deluxe and two-room suites with microwaves, refrigerators and in-room coffee makers, indoor/outdoor swimming pool, indoor Jacuzzi; non-smoking rooms available.

At Drury Inn you'll enjoy clean, comfortable rooms where the quality is consistent and the decor is fresh. The king deluxe and two-room suites feature microwaves, refrigerators and in-room coffee makers. The inn offers an indoor/outdoor swimming pool with sundeck and indoor Jacuzzi and exercise room.

Start your day with the complimentary Quickstart breakfast of fresh fruits, bagels, pastries, juices, hot and cold cereals, toast, milk, coffee and tea.

Local attractions close by include White Water, Six Flags, Cumberland Mall and Historic Marietta.

Ramada Limited Suites

Ramada Limited Suites
630 Franklin Road
Marietta, GA 30067
800-2-RAMADA ▪ (770) 919-7878

Room Rates:	$44–$57, including continental breakfast. AAA and AARP discounts.
Pet Charges or Deposits:	$10 per stay; $25 refundable deposit.
Rated: 3 Paws 🐾🐾🐾	45 spacious suites with microwaves, refrigerators, in-room coffee makers, pull-out sofa beds, writing desks, in-room movies, some Jacuzzi and kitchenette rooms, outdoor pool, nonsmoking rooms, children stay free.

When looking for home-away-from-home accommodations for your next business trip or family vacation, the Ramada Limited Suites may be the choice for you. Your spacious suite will have a microwave, refrigerator and in-room coffee maker, perfect for families on the run. There is even the added convenience of a pull-out sofa bed in the sitting area for extra sleeping space. There are large writing desks that double as dining tables, remote-control television and in-room movies to entertain the children. Some of the suites have the additional luxury of an in-room Jacuzzi and a kitchenette. All guests receive a complimentary continental breakfast to start the day.

The inn is centrally located to many restaurants, the White Water park, Six Flags amusement park, Marietta business district, Marietta Convention Center, the Georgia Dome, Atlanta Zoo, Braves stadium and several other area attractions. The spacious grounds are perfect for a morning or evening stroll with your dog.

Amberley Suite Hotel

Amberley Suite Hotel
5885 Oakbrook Parkway
Norcross, GA 30093
800-365-0659 ▪ (770) 263-0515

Room Rates:	$69–$129
Pet Charges or Deposits:	$50 refundable deposit. Manager's approval required.
Rated: 4 Paws 🐾🐾🐾🐾	177 executive rooms, one- or two-bedroom suites or apartments with refrigerator and coffee maker, some with kitchenettes or full kitchens; pool, sauna, whirlpool, exercise room, restaurant and cocktail lounge.

Conveniently located in Norcross, near Atlanta, is the Amberley Suite Hotel. Relax in the comfortable well-appointed rooms, suites or apartments.

Health-conscious travelers will appreciate the fitness center, where they can have a good workout, relax in the Swedish sauna or swim a few laps in the outdoor pool.

The elegant Watson's Café and Lounge serves breakfast and luncheon buffets and an evening menu. The Fireplace Lobby is the perfect place to spend time relaxing with a morning cup of coffee or meeting friends for an evening cocktail.

Quality Inn

Quality Inn
Interstate 75 at US 341
Perry, GA 31069
800-422-1345 ▪ (912) 987-1345

Room Rates:	$50–$75, including continental breakfast. AAA and AARP discounts.
Pet Charges or Deposits:	$5 per day.
Rated: 3 Paws 🐾🐾🐾	69 rooms and 2 large suites with coffee makers, television, air conditioning, some with microwaves and refrigerators, restaurant and cocktail lounge, swimming pool, outdoor playground and 13 acres of grounds with gardens and ponds.

Built with the guests' comfort in mind, the Quality Inn of Perry offers charming Early American-style furnished rooms in a peaceful garden setting. The inn is one mile from the state Agricenter, which hosts dog shows several times each year.

You and your pets will no doubt want to take time to stroll the inn's serene gardens, one of the most photographed spots in all of Georgia, with flowers in bloom all year long, delightful goldfish ponds, the Bamboo Tea House with ferns and exotic plants and the lovely Four Seasons Garden, with its mature trees, sculptured bushes and charming brick walkways. A 1855 plantation house, home to the inn's owner, is situated in the lush gardens as well.

There is also an inviting outdoor pool and playground area, located in the garden, where children of all ages can enjoy the sparkling blue water and adjacent playground equipment, or visit one of many area attractions and parks.

Royal Windsor Cottage

Royal Windsor Cottage
4490 Highway 356
Sautee, GA 30571
(706) 878-1322

Room Rates: **$95–$145**, including full breakfast.
Pet Charges or Deposits: **$10** per stay. Small dogs only. Manager's approval required.
Rated: 4 Paws 🐾🐾🐾🐾 4 English-style guest rooms with private baths, furnished in antiques, down comforters, central air and heat, large porches, English breakfast and afternoon tea.

S
ituated on 22 wooded acres near the Unicoi State Park and Anna Ruby Falls is the lovely Royal Windsor Cottage. Featured in *Southern Living* magazine, this tasteful English-style cottage brings a touch of Old England to the South by re-establishing the philosophy of being pampered.

Guests will find four distinctive, beautifully decorated rooms to choose from, all with private baths, queen-sized beds, lovely linens and down comforters and a private balcony to enjoy the magnificent mountain views.

Your day will begin with a traditional fireside English breakfast served on fine china with sterling silver cutlery in the dining room, or out on the large porch, where guests are encouraged to "sit a spell" and relax in true Southern tradition.

You and your dog will enjoy exploring the 22 wooded acres of property before heading out for a day of hiking, fishing, swimming or picnicking at Unicoi State Park. Make sure you return to the cottage in time to enjoy English tea and crumpets.

Joan's on Jones Bed and Breakfast

Joan's on Jones Bed and Breakfast
17 West Jones Street
Savannah, GA 31401
800-407-3863 ▪ (912) 234-3863

Room Rates:	$115–$130, including continental breakfast.
Pet Charges or Deposits:	$50 per stay; room rate as deposit. No cats, please.
Rated: 3 Paws 🐾🐾🐾	2 luxury suites with private sitting rooms, private baths, kitchen or kitchenette, one with fireplace and off-street parking.

J oan's on Jones Bed and Breakfast is a charming 1883 Victorian townhouse set in the heart of Savannah's National Historic Landmark District. Here guests can relax in Victorian splendor surrounded by an array of antiques, offering a glimpse into an elegant past.

The splendid Jones Street Suite, with its private front parlor and sliding pocket doors leading into the charming bedroom with a four-poster, carved rice bed—normally reserved for the head of the plantation—also comes with a kitchenette, fresh fruit and wine to make you feel welcome. The Garden Suite has a secluded, walled garden, heady with the lush scent of Southern plantings, accompanied by the tinkling sounds of the splashing garden fountain, only steps from your sunny, private sitting room, and a sleeping area with a queen-sized iron bed and period furnishings and a large fireplace once used for cooking. If you wish, you may prepare your own breakfast in the suite's full kitchen; all the fixings will be provided.

You and your dog can take advantage of the central location near several city squares and all the interesting sites in the National Historic Landmark District.

Culpepper House Bed and Breakfast

Culpepper House Bed and Breakfast
35 Broad Street
Senoia, GA 30276
(770) 599-8182

Room Rates:	$85, including a full breakfast. AAA, AARP, AKC and ABA discounts.
Pet Charges or Deposits:	None. Manager's approval required.
Rated: 3 Paws 🐾🐾🐾	3 guest rooms furnished in period antiques and reproductions with private baths.

Step back 120 years to the gracious Victorian elegance of the Culpepper House Bed and Breakfast. Set among lovely old oak trees, this charming inn still has its original woodwork, reminiscent of the Steamboat Gothic style. The architectural theme begins with the wraparound porch, and is carried throughout the house in the trimwork and staircases, the stained glass windows in the stairwell, the original light fixtures and massive sliding pocket doors leading into the parlor. This fully restored inn showcases period antiques and wonderful reproductions on heart-pine floors amid a backdrop of massive 12-foot ceilings.

Enjoy a four-poster, canopy bed next to a fireplace, with sounds of the night coming through the window. Wake to a gourmet breakfast, then take a tandem bike ride through the historic town, visiting area shops and the picturesque countryside, or just sit on the porch and rock.

The Statesboro Inn and Restaurant

The Statesboro Inn and Restaurant
106 South Main Street
Statesboro, GA 30453
800-846-9466 ▪ (912) 489-8628

Room Rates:	$75–$120, including full breakfast. AAA and AARP discounts.
Pet Charges or Deposits:	None. Manager's approval required.
Rated: 4 Paws 🐾🐾🐾🐾	18 guest rooms and 1 luxury suite, all with private baths, whirlpool tubs, ceiling fans, remote-control televisions, furnished with antiques, featuring fireplaces, private entrances, screened porches and restaurant.

Built in 1904, the Statesboro Inn and Restaurant integrates the elements of late Victorian bay windows and gables with the Neoclassical features of the Palladian entry and Tuscan columns. The beautifully decorated rooms are furnished with antiques, working fireplaces and private bathrooms with whirlpool tubs.

Guests may relax and enjoy a good book on their private porch or retire to the parlor and visit with other guests. The homey feeling of this country inn has been combined with modern amenities to make your stay an experience to remember. Located on the property is the Hattie Holloway cabin where Georgia Music Hall of Fame member "Blind Willie" is said to have written "Statesboro Blues," made famous by the Allman Brothers Band.

The Inn's "Three Diamond" public dining room is renowned for its atmosphere of casual but elegant dining, offering an ever-evolving Continental and regional menu. The restaurant features many old family recipes and makes its own breads and desserts fresh daily.

The Coleman House Inn

The Coleman House Inn
323 North Main Street
Swainsboro, GA 30401
(912) 237-9100

Room Rates:	$55–$85, including continental breakfast.
Pet Charges or Deposits:	None
Rated: 4 Paws 🐾🐾🐾🐾	7 guest rooms with private baths and showers, antiques, cable television, telephones, individually controlled heat and air conditioning.

T he Coleman House Inn is a picturesque, three-story clapboard, turn-of-the-century Victorian bed and breakfast inn, eclectically combining the Queen Anne and Neoclassical Revival styles of decor that are commonly found in Georgia.

Your accommodations are furnished with charming antiques that include a cozy queen, double or twin bed as well as a private bath with footed tub and shower.

This was the first house in Emanuel County to have indoor plumbing and electricity. The front parlor exhibits many Victorian characteristics, such as wooden floors, high ceilings, large pocket doors and bay windows. The grand inn has 11 fireplaces, a central tower projecting from the roof, which includes a balcony and a lovely veranda that surrounds the building's facade, inviting guests to sit down, relax with their dog, sip a glass of iced tea and enjoy the best that Southern hospitality has to offer.

Holiday Inn

Holiday Inn
1725 Memorial Drive
Waycross, GA 31501
800-HOLIDAY ▪ (912) 283-4490

Room Rates:	$45–$60, including full breakfast buffet. AARP discount. Tour packages available.
Pet Charges or Deposits:	None. Small pets only.
Rated: 3 Paws 🐾🐾🐾	145 guest rooms and 3 spacious suites, all with cable television, free in-room movies, some with balconies, refrigerators, safes, putting green, pool, exercise room, playground, valet laundry, airport transportation, restaurant and cocktail lounge.

T he Holiday Inn is centrally located in the city of Waycross, in the Coastal Plains of southeast Georgia, near "America's Nature Wonderland," the world-famous Okefenokee Swamp Park. The park is said to be one of America's most unique and beautiful wilderness areas. The inn offers tour packages that include your room rate, full breakfast buffet, plus admission to the Okefenokee Swamp Park. The six-hour tour package includes a one-hour Deep Swamp Boat Tour and a one-hour guided tour aboard the "Olympic Tram," which takes you deep into the heart of the swamp.

At Holiday Inn, you will find comfortable accommodations featuring spacious rooms and suites with cable television and free in-room movies. Some rooms have balconies overlooking the patio and pool areas, plus the added convenience of in-room refrigerators and safes. Guests are invited to partake of the complimentary full breakfast buffet before heading out for the day.

WHERE TO TAKE YOUR PET IN
Georgia

Please Note: *Pets must be on a leash at all times and may be restricted to certain areas. For directions, use fees, pet charges and general information, contact the numbers listed below.*

National Forest General Information

U.S. Forest Service
1720 Peachtree Road, NW
Atlanta, GA 30367

800-280-2267 – reservations
(404) 347-2384 – information

National Forest and National Recreational Areas

ATLANTA

Chattahoochee River National Recreational Area, north of Atlanta, offers 4,100 acres of parkland, day-use trails, canoeing, kayaking and rafting, small motor boats, boat rentals and shuttle services. There are picnic areas, bicycle and hiking trails, fishing, swimming and nature programs. For more information, call (770) 399-8070 or 952-4419.

CHATSWORTH

Chattahoochee and Oconee National Forests, located in Northern Georgia, encompass 749,268 acres, plus 113,100 acres of the Oconee National Forest in Central Georgia. The Cohutta Wilderness covers 35,307 acres and has hiking, fishing, camping, picnic areas, hiking trails, boat ramps for boating, fishing, swimming, a visitors' center, wilderness areas and the Chattooga National Wild and Scenic River. For more information, call (770) 536-0541.

FOLKSTON

Suwannee Canal Recreation Area, 8 miles southwest on SR 23 and SR 121, then continue for 3.5 miles west on Spur. The 396,000-acre area includes a restored swamp homestead and a 4,000-foot boardwalk which leads to a 50-foot observation tower. The area also offers boat and canoe trips, bicycle rentals, fishing, swimming areas, picnic areas, nature programs and a visitors center. For more information, call (912) 496-7156 or 800-792-6796.

Army Corps Of Engineers
Parks and Recreational Areas

AUGUSTA

J. Strom Thurmond Lake, located 20 miles northwest of Augusta on SR 28, encompasses 70,000 acres. You will find camping, picnic areas, hiking and bicycling trails, a boat ramp for boating, boat rentals, fishing, swimming, nature programs and a visitors' center.

BUFORD

Lake Sidney Lanier occupies 56,000 acres of parkland with camping, picnic areas, hiking trails, a boat ramp for boating, boat rentals, swimming, fishing, nature programs and a visitors' center.

CARTERSVILLE

Allatoona Lake, located 6 miles southeast of Cartersville off Interstate 75, encompasses 25,806 acres offers visitors campsites, a boat ramp for boating, water skiing, fishing, swimming, beaches, hiking trails, picnic areas, a nature program and a visitors' center. For more information, call (770) 382-4700.

ELBERTON

Richard B. Russell Lake, 20 miles east of Elberton on SR 72, encompasses 26,500 acres. You will find campsites, picnic areas, hiking trails, a boat ramp for boating, boat rentals, nature programs and a visitors' center.

FORT GAINES

Lake Walter F. George, located 2 miles north of Fort Gaines off SR 72, occupies 45,000 acres. It has camping, picnic areas, hiking and bicycling trails, a boat ramp for boating, boat rentals, fishing, swimming, nature programs and a visitors' center. For more information, call (912) 768-2934.

WEST POINT

West Point Lake, located 4 miles north of town off US Highway 29, is a 25,900-acre man-made lake offering camping, picnicking, hiking trails, a boat ramp for boating, fishing, swimming, a nature program and a visitors' center.

HARTWELL

Hartwell Lake, located 6 miles north of Hartwell on US 29, encompasses 56,000 acres and offers visitors 962 miles of shoreline, campsites, picnic areas, a boat ramp for boating, a marina, boat rentals, fishing, swimming, nature programs and a visitors' center. For more information, call (706) 376-4788.

State Park General Information

Georgia State Parks and
Historic Sites
Department of Natural Resources
Communications Office
205 Butler Street, SE, Suite 1258
Atlanta, GA 30334

800-864-7275 – camping
reservations
(404) 656-3530 – information

State Parks

ADEL

Reed Bingham State Park, located 6 miles west of Adel off SR 37, has 1,620 acres of parkland surrounding a 375-acre lake. Known for its boating and water skiing, there are also nature trails, campsites, picnic areas, swimming and fishing. For more information, call (912) 896-3551.

APPLING

Mistletoe State Park, 10 miles north of Appling off SR 150, has 1,920 acres of parkland offering campsites, picnic areas, a boat ramp, boat rentals, fishing, swimming, hiking trails and a nature program. For more information, call (706) 541-0321.

BLAKELY

Kolomoki Mounds State Park, located 6 miles north of town off US Highway 27, has 1,293 acres of parkland. You will find a museum, camping facilities, picnic areas, hiking trails, boat ramps for boating, rental boats, fishing, swimming, a nature program and a visitors' center. For more information, call (912) 723-5296 for the park or 723-3396 for the museum.

CARTERSVILLE

Red Top Mountain State Park is located 2 miles east of Interstate 75; take the Red Top exit. This 1,950-acre park along Lake Allatoona offers miniature golf, tennis courts, water skiing, campsites, picnic areas, hiking trails, a boat ramp and marina, fishing and swimming. For more information, call (770) 975-0055.

DAHLONEGA

Amicalola Falls State Park, located 15 miles west of Dahlonega on SR 52 near SR 183, has 1,020 acres of parkland with campsites, picnic areas, hiking trails, fishing, swimming, nature programs and a visitors' center. For more information, call (706) 864-3711.

DONALSONVILLE

Seminole State Park, located 16 miles south of Donalsonville off SR 39, consists of 343 acres of parkland located on 37,500-acre Lake Seminole. You will find campsites, picnic areas, hiking trails, a boat ramp for boating, great fishing, swimming and water skiing. For more information, call (912) 861-3137.

DOUGLAS

General Coffee State Park, 6 miles east of Douglas on SR 32, is 1,490 acres of parkland combining natural, recreational and historical resources in one park. Along with wildlife, endangered plants and agricultural history, visitors will find a heritage farm, camping facilities, picnic areas, hiking trails and a lake for swimming and fishing. For more information, call (912) 384-7082.

HELEN

Unicoi State Park, located 2 miles northeast of Helen via SR 356, encompasses 1,801 acres nestled in the Georgia mountains. You will find campsites, picnic areas, hiking and bicycling trails, tennis, fishing, swimming and nature programs. For more information, call(706) 878-2201.

JACKSON

Indian Springs State Park, located 5 miles southeast of Jackson on SR 42 off US Highway 23, is a 523-acre park that contains a mineral spring. There is a museum, camping facilities, picnic areas, a boat ramp, fishing, swimming and a visitors' center. For more information, call (770) 504-2277.

LAVONIA

Tugaloo State Park, located 6 miles north of Lavonia off SR 328, is a 393-acre park on a rugged peninsula jutting into 55,500-acre Lake Hartwell. There are camping sites, water skiing, swimming, beaches, boating, tennis, and nature trails for hiking. For more information, call (706) 356-4362.

LUMPKIN

Providence Canyon State Conservation Park is Georgia's "Little Grand Canyon." Visitors will find picnic facilities, trails leading up to the rim of the canyon and places where backpackers can stay overnight in the back country. For more information, call (912) 838-6202.

McRAE

Little Ocmulgee State Park, located 2 miles north of McRae on US 441, has 1,397 acres of parkland offering an 18-hole golf course, a lake, nature trails, camping, tennis, a boat ramp for boating, water skiing, fishing and picnic areas. For more information, call (912) 868-7474 or (912) 868-6651 for golf.

MILLEN

Magnolia Springs State Park, located 5 miles north of Millen on US 25, has 948 acres of parkland, including crystal clear springs. There are campsites, picnic areas, hiking trails, a boat ramp, fishing, swimming, an aquarium and nature trails. For more information, call (912) 982-1660.

RICHMOND HILL

Fort McAllister State Historic Park, located 10 miles east on US Highway 17, then east on SR 144 to 144 Spur, consists of 1,690 acres on the bank of the Great Ogeechee River. There are exhibits of artillery and a history of the fort in the museum, as well as campsites, cabins, picnic areas, a boat ramp for boating and swimming areas. For more information, call (912) 727-2339.

RUTLEDGE

Hard Labor Creek State Park, 2 miles north of Rutledge off Interstate 20, consists of 5,805 acres and includes an 18-hole golf course, camping facilities, picnic areas, swimming, beach front, horse trails, a boat ramp for boating, fishing, hiking and a visitors' center. For more information, call (706) 557-3001.

SAVANNAH

Skidaway Island State Park, located 6 miles southeast of Savannah, off Interstate 16 to SR 21, consists of 506 acres of parkland with camping facilities, a swimming pool, nature trails, picnic areas, a boat ramp for boating, fishing and a visitors' center. For more information, call (912) 598-2300.

TWIN CITY

George L. Smith State Park located 4 miles southeast of Twin City off SR 23, encompasses 1,355 acres with a grist mill and covered bridge. Visitors will find a lake with a boat ramp for fishing, canoeing and boating, picnic areas and camping. For more information, call (912) 763-763-2759.

WINDER

Fort Yargo State Park, 1 mile south of Winder on SR 81, is an 1,850-acre historic park. This park features camping, fishing, picnic areas, a playground, hiking trails, a boat ramp for boating, boat rentals, swimming, nature programs, and a visitors' center. For more information, call (770) 867-3489.

Louisiana

71
167
165
Lake Providence
Shreveport
Monroe
Grambling
20
Tallulah
49
65
Winnfield
Natchitoches
84
Alexandria
171
165
St. Francisville
55
49
Ville Platte
190
Baton Rouge
10
Lake Charles
Lafayette
10
New Orleans
Slidell
New Iberia
90
Houma
Stephensville
Bourg

Mississippi River

PETS WELCOME!

Louisiana

Three Dog Bakery

This unique "bakery for dogs" with murals of canines adorning the walls, serves up all-natural treats and gifts for the pampered pooch.

Three Dog Bakery, located at 827 Royal Street in New Orleans, features baked goods made specifically for dogs, such as "boxer brownies" "puptarts" and "paw-lines." Favorite cookie requests are the Big Scary Kitties, which are cat-shaped peanut butter cookies half dipped in carob, and Ciao Wow Cheese Pizzas—crispy pizzas with homemade tomato sauce, topped with low fat Parmesan cheese and oregano. Snickerpoodles are cookies with a touch of honey and ground cinnamon, embossed with a poodle on each and the favored Sarah's Slab O'Ribs is Kansas-city-style ribs, slow roasted with a sauce of fresh tomatoes, molasses, honey, garlic and herbs.

This shop also carries gift items such as treat jars and special bowls, and it bakes up specialty cakes for birthdays and obedience school graduations.

Celebrities such as Julie Andrews, Delta Burke, Trent Reznor and the cast of "The Big Easy" can be found here, feeding their dogs these all-natural treats.

Le Jardin Sur Le Bayou

Le Jardin Sur Le Bayou
256 Lower Country Drive
Bourg, LA 70343
(504) 594-2722

Room Rates: $85, including a gourmet breakfast and garden tour.
Pet Charges or Deposits: Call for deposit.
Rated: 5 Paws 🐾🐾🐾🐾🐾 Private upstairs suite with sitting room and private bath.

Enjoy Cajun hospitality on this 26-acre registered wildlife sanctuary featuring century-old live oaks and native plants teeming with hummingbirds and butterflies. Stroll quiet garden paths under an oak canopy, pause at bridges and enjoy goldfish ponds, swing, or just sit on a garden bench and watch the extensive variety of birds.

Inside the inn awaits a comfortable and tastefully decorated private upstairs suite, set back from a quiet country road, offering central air and heat, cable television, telephone, refrigerator and use of screened breezeway and laundry facilities. Owners and innkeepers Dave and Jo Ann Cognet create magical breakfasts each morning that are served in the garden, overlooking the fish ponds.

This highly recommended bed and breakfast inn is located just one hour from New Orleans. Consider staying at least two nights to enjoy the home cooking and garden tour.

Maison des Anges Bed and Breakfast

Maison des Anges Bed and Breakfast
508 Academy Street
Houma, LA 70360
(504) 873-7662

Room Rates:	$55–$80, including a full breakfast.
Pet Charges or Deposits:	$10 per day; first-night room rate as deposit.
Rated: 4 Paws 🐾🐾🐾🐾	5 guest rooms with semi-private and private baths, king, double and twin-sized beds, telephone, cable television with remote control, laundry facilities and small fenced courtyard.

Built in 1904 for J.C. Cunningham, former mayor of Houma, the Maison des Anges Bed and Breakfast was the first Victorian-style home in Houma. Located near the downtown area, the inn is within walking distance to the Mardi Gras parade route and other historical points of interest. Except for the more recent addition to the home, the building was constructed of virgin cypress, including the interior and exterior walls. Each post of the porch was turned from one solid timber and bears the stencil "St. Louis Cypress Co." under the original green paint.

The house features five guest rooms, two of which may be combined into a two-bedroom suite, with private and semi-private baths with the original claw-foot bathtubs and hand painted tiles. There is a spacious, common sun room with cable television and a VCR for guests to use, plus a large fully equipped kitchen, spacious dining room where you can enjoy your complimentary breakfast, as well as a comfortable smoking area. The small fenced courtyard is perfect for exercising the dog.

Bois des Chênes Bed and Breakfast Inn

Bois des Chênes Bed and Breakfast Inn
338 North Sterling
Lafayette, LA 70501
(318) 233-7816

Room Rates:	$95–$125, full breakfast included.
Pet Charges or Deposits:	$10 per stay, $50 deposit. Manager's approval required. No cats, please.
Rated: 4 Paws 🐾🐾🐾🐾	7 suites with private baths, some private sitting rooms and wood-burning fireplaces, complimentary breakfast and wine.

S ituated near the center of Lafayette is the award-winning Bois des Chênes Bed and Breakfast Inn, part of the Charles Mouton Plantation House. This magnificent plantation managed to survive the Civil War and is now on the National Register of Historic Places. Over the years, it has become an important entity in the culture and history of the city.

Built in 1820, this Acadian-style plantation house has been lovingly restored and graced with period antiques of mainly Louisiana French origin, as well as American pieces to complement this unique architectural design. Guests may choose their accommodations from the Main Plantation House, which offers two charming suites with sitting rooms and private baths. One suite offers a cozy, wood-burning fireplace. The 1890 Carriage House is at the rear of the plantation and features three suites upstairs and two downstairs, all with private baths and period antiques, yet still affording modern conveniences such as a television and refrigerator.

La Quinta Inn

La Quinta Inn
1035 US 165 Bypass South
Monroe, LA 71203
800-NU-ROOMS ▪ (318) 322-3900

Room Rates:	$57–$70, including continental breakfast. AAA and AARP discounts.
Pet Charges or Deposits:	None. Manager's approval required. No long-haired pets, please.
Rated: 3 Paws 🐾🐾🐾	129 spacious rooms and 1 luxury suite, all with king-sized beds, 25-inch televisions with expanded television channels, free airport shuttle, 24-hour front desk services, laundry and dry cleaning services.

The spacious, quiet rooms, oversized bathrooms and large work areas make La Quinta Inn a versatile place to stay. The inn's "Make yourself at home" motto is reflected in its large televisions, expanded selection of channels, first-run movies, hot new video games and home-like decor.

A complimentary "Light Breakfast," featuring your choice of cereal, fresh fruit, bagels, pastries, juice, milk and coffee, is included in your room rate. The inn also offers a heated outdoor swimming pool and beautifully landscaped grounds to enjoy with your canine pal.

La Quinta Inn is located near the Louisiana Purchase Gardens and Zoo, Northeast Louisiana University, Masur Museum of Art and Antique Alley.

The Chimes Bed and Breakfast of New Orleans

The Chimes Bed and Breakfast of New Orleans
1146 Constantinople
New Orleans, LA 70115
800-729-4640 ▪ (504) 488-4640

Room Rates:	$79–$135, including continental breakfast.
Pet Charges or Deposits:	$5 per stay. Manager's approval required.
Rated: 3 Paws 🐾🐾🐾	3 air-conditioned guest rooms and 2 large suites with private entrances opening onto the courtyard.

Uptown in the largest historical neighborhood in the United States is The Chimes Bed and Breakfast of New Orleans. This 1876 inn offers guests individually decorated rooms reflecting the flavor of New Orleans, with private entries, beautiful antique iron beds, claw-foot bathtubs, high ceilings, wooden or slate floors and a friendly atmosphere. The first-floor rooms have large French doors that open onto an old brick courtyard full of tropical plants to shade you while you relax or read in the hammock.

Begin your day with a lavish continental breakfast served in the large dining room. Only minutes from the famed French Quarter, the inn's neighborhood of ante-bellum homes will take you back in time. It is a charming route for you and your dog to take for a leisurely stroll. You can even get a little help with dog-walking duties if you ask.

Three blocks from St. Charles Avenue, The Chimes is minutes away from major New Orleans attractions including the Audubon Zoological Gardens, antique shops and the famous restaurants, jazz clubs and art galleries.

Essem's House — New Orleans' First Bed and Breakfast

Essem's House — New Orleans' First Bed and Breakfast
3660 Gentilly Boulevard
New Orleans, LA 70122
800-240-0070 ▪ (504) 947-3401

Room Rates:	$55–$75, including continental breakfast.
Pet Charges or Deposits:	Call for deposit.
Rated: 3 Paws 🐾🐾🐾	Private guest cottage with separate living area, king or twin beds, kitchen and bath, plus 3 guest rooms, one with a private bath, featuring king and double beds, televisions, refrigerators, off-street parking, exercise area for pets.

 tree-lined, shaded boulevard leads to the charming Essem's House — New Orleans' First Bed and Breakfast. A continental breakfast is included in your room rate.

This charming brick home offers guests their choice of the large master bedroom with its striking rose, black and ivory decor, featuring a king-sized bed and a private bath. The other two guest rooms may be made into a suite or rented separately. Both rooms have double beds with a large bathroom situated between the two rooms. The private guest cottage features a king-sized bed or two twin beds, a living area, kitchen and bath.

Guests are welcome to enjoy the living room and solarium area to relax with a good book or enjoy the warmth of a crackling fire. The residential setting invites an evening stroll.

Hilton Riverside Hotel

Hilton Riverside Hotel
2 Poydras Street
New Orleans, LA 70140
800-HILTONS ▪ (504) 561-0500

Room Rates:	$240 and up.
Pet Charges or Deposits:	None. Manager's approval required.
Rated: 4 Paws 🐾🐾🐾🐾	1,522 guest rooms and 78 luxury suites, some with wet bars, two swimming pools, racquet and health club, international shopping mall, full-service salon, laundry/valet services, limousine service to the airport, Riverboat Flamingo Casino, restaurants, coffee shop and cocktail lounge.

Towering above the banks of the Mississippi River, near the famed French Quarter, the Riverwalk Festival Marketplace and Hilton's Flamingo Casino, is the Hilton Riverside Hotel. This 29-story structure features 1,600 soundproof guest rooms.

The Hilton's RiverCenter Racquet and Health Club is a complete facility boasting four racquetball courts, three squash courts, a golf studio and a basketball court. The exercise complex features Nautilus equipment, Stairmasters and treadmills, plus a tanning salon, aerobics studio, massage-therapy, saunas and whirlpools.

Hilton's newest amenity, the Flamingo Casino is accessible from the hotel's Riverside lobby. This grand attraction features more than 1,400 slot and video machines, along with roulette, craps and blackjack.

Choices for entertainment and dining are plentiful at the Hilton.

New Orleans Accommodations Reservation Service

New Orleans Accommodations Reservation Service
PO Box 8163
New Orleans, LA 70005
888-240-0070 ▪ (504) 838-0071

Room Rates: $55–$350, some include full or continental breakfast.
Pet Charges or Deposits: None. No cats, please. Manager's approval required.
Rated: 3 to 5 Paws Bed and breakfast inns, condos, homestays and apartments. Call for individual amenities.

I f you are looking for something different from the usual hotel accommodations when visiting the New Orleans area, try booking your reservations through the New Orleans Accommodations Reservation Service. You will learn of hosted or unhosted accommodations in outstanding homes, inns, apartments and guest cottages. Each property is carefully evaluated before allowing it to become a part of the service. Most accommodations are air-conditioned and are located near public transportation to get you to the French Quarter and the downtown area in minutes.

Rates quoted are for double occupancy and are based on the type of accommodation, location, private or shared baths. Make sure to tell them that you are bringing your dog and mention any special amenities you may need, such as a park nearby or an exercise yard. And, of course, all major credit cards are accepted.

La Quinta Inn

La Quinta Inn
794 East I-10 Service Road
Slidell, LA 70461
800-NU-ROOMS ▪ (504) 643-9770

Room Rates:	$59–$99, including a continental breakfast. AAA and AARP discounts.
Pet Charges or Deposits:	None. Pets up to 50 lbs. Manager's approval required.
Rated: 3 Paws 🐾🐾🐾	177 spacious rooms and 5 luxury suites, all with king-sized beds, 25-inch television, coffee maker, in-room movies, 24-hour front desk services, laundry facilities, dry cleaning services, heated outdoor pool and spa.

T he La Quinta Inn offers families on vacation and business travelers all the comforts and conveniences of home at a reasonable price. From the oversized bathrooms and the large work areas with dataport phones, to the comfortable recliners and king-sized beds featured in all the rooms, the accommodations are suitable for a week or a weekend. You and your dog will enjoy walking the spacious landscaped grounds.

Start your day off with the complimentary First Light breakfast, featuring your choice of cereals, fresh fruit, pastries, bagels, juice, milk and coffee, before heading out for the day.

Relax by the heated pool, soak in the whirlpool, work out in the fully equipped fitness room or visit one of the regional attractions. Such attractions include swamp tours, casinos, vineyards, antique and outlet shopping, a Mardi Gras mask factory and New Orleans' famed French Quarter.

Butler Greenwood Plantation

Butler Greenwood Plantation
8345 U.S. Highway 61
St. Francisville, LA 70775
(504) 635-6312

Room Rates:	$100–$110, including continental breakfast and tour of main house.
Pet Charges or Deposits:	None. Manager's approval required.
Rated: 4 Paws ❀ ❀ ❀ ❀	6 cottages with air conditioning, fireplaces, kitchens, library, laundry facilities, swimming pool, Jacuzzi, and tennis court.

Built in 1796, this well-loved working plantation boasts a main ante-bellum house with six charming cottages, all set among 2,200 acres. The extensive grounds have hundreds of ancient, moss-draped oak trees and ante-bellum gardens. All guests receive a guided tour of the grounds and main house with historical information by direct descendants of the original builder.

The 19th-century cottages include the Cook's Cottage with claw-foot tub, fireplace and a porch swing overlooking the duck pond. The Gazebo is a six-sided building with three 9-foot-tall antique stained-glass church windows and a king-sized bed. The Pond House sleeps six and has a hammock on the shaded porch overlooking the pond. The Treehouse is at the edge of a steep, wooded ravine with a three-level deck, king-sized cypress four-poster bed and a fireplace. The Dovecote is three stories with sloped, shingled sides; it sleeps six, has a fireplace, a Jacuzzi and a deck on the ravine.

Take advantage of the spacious acreage to take your dog on a long hike and observe nature at its finest.

Lake Rosemound Inn

Lake Rosemound Inn
10473 Lindsey Lane
St. Francisville, LA 70775
(504) 635-3176

Room Rates:	$75–$105, including full breakfast.
Pet Charges or Deposits:	None. Manager's approval required.
Rated: 4 Paws 🐾🐾🐾🐾	4 guest rooms and 2 luxurious suites with Jacuzzi tubs, ceiling fans, television, fireplaces, private entrances, clubhouse room with ice cream parlor, set on three lakefront acres.

Perched on three beautiful acres and bound on two sides by Lake Rosemound, one of the most picturesque areas in Louisiana, is charming Lake Rosemound Inn. This romantic inn features the Rosemound and Feliciana Suites, with Jacuzzi tubs, and the Sunrise and Sunset rooms with magnificent views of the lake.

Guests may choose to relax in the Clubhouse Parlor, complete with dart boards, television, stereo, a Brunswick pool table and the inn's famous "help yourself" ice cream parlor. The common kitchen is complete with grill, refrigerator and microwave. All rooms have television, telephone, queen-sized beds and private baths.

Start your morning with a big country breakfast before you head out to the dock for a day of fishing, stroll along the shoreline with your dog, bike the rolling hills or take in the abundant wildlife that graces the property.

Cajun Houseboat Rentals

Cajun Houseboat Rentals
Docked in Stephensville
Mailing address:
613 Sixth Street
Morgan City, LA 70380
(504) 385-2738

Room Rates:	$95 plus $10 per person, per day. Weekly rates available.
Pet Charges or Deposits:	$47.50 deposit. Manager's approval required.
Rated: 3 Paws 🐾🐾🐾	2-bedroom houseboat that sleeps 8, towels and bedding supplied, full bath with shower, fully equipped kitchen, central air and heat, covered veranda on private dock, barbecue pit, picnic table, laundry facilities, TV, stereo, VCR, telephone, located near stores.

Permanently docked in the heart of Stephensville on Bayou Long near Morgan City, you'll find Cajun Houseboat Rentals' Magnolia houseboat. This authentic Cajun house on water allows you to have all the conveniences of home as you experience the tranquil beauty and abundant natural wildlife of the bayous.

You can even fish for dinner off your own porch. Everything is supplied for you except your food, but you are only a short distance from restaurants featuring local cuisine, grocery stores and seafood markets, just in case the fish aren't biting. Spend the day enjoying water sports, zooming across the water on a Jet Ski or sailboard, relaxing on the beach or hiking around the shore with your dog. If you wish, you may bring your own boat to tour the bayou or take one of the guided fishing trips. In the evening, join locals at the "chanky-chank," where you can dance to hot Cajun music.

WHERE TO TAKE YOUR PET IN
Louisiana

Please Note: *Pets must be on a leash at all times and may be restricted to certain areas. For directions, use fees, pet charges and general information, contact the numbers listed below.*

National Forest General Information

Kisatchie National Forest
PO Box 5500
Pineville, LA 71361

800-280-2267 – camping reservations
(318) 473-7160 – information

National Forests

HOMER

Kisatchie National Forest, located in both central and northern Louisiana near Minden, consists of 600,000 acres of national forest, including Caney Lakes Recreation Area and Cane National Recreational Trail. There are camping facilities, picnic areas, hiking and bicycle trails, a boat ramp for boating, fishing and swimming. For more information, call (318) 927-2061.

State Parks General Information

Louisiana Office of State Parks   (504) 342-8111
Dept. of Culture, Recreation and Tourism
PO Drawer 1111
Baton Rouge, LA 70821

State Parks

FRANKLIN

Cypremort Point State Park, 24 miles south of Jeanerette off SR 319, has 185 acres. The area is perfect for crabbing, water skiing and windsurfing. It also has picnic areas, a boat ramp for boating, fishing and swimming. For more information, call (318) 867-4510.

LAKE CHARLES

Sam Houston Jones State Park, located 9 miles north of Lake Charles off SR 378, encompasses 1,068 acres of parkland where three rivers flow together. Visitors will find camping facilities, picnic areas, hiking trails, and a boat ramp for boating and fishing. For more information, call (318) 855-2665.

MANDEVILLE

Fountainebleau State Park, 3 miles southeast of Mandeville on US 190, takes in 2,700 acres on the north shore of Lake Pontchartrain. You will find camping, picnic areas, a swimming pool, hiking trails, and a boat ramp for boating and fishing. For more information, call (504) 624-4443.

POYDRAS

St. Bernard State Park, located 18 miles southeast of New Orleans on Highway 39 South, consists of 358 acres on the Mississippi River, with camping facilities, picnic areas, hiking trails, boat rentals, fishing and swimming. For more information, call (504) 682-2101.

ST. JOSEPH

Lake Bruin State Park, 3 miles northeast of St. Joseph on SR 605, consists of a 53-acre park on the shore of the 3,500-acre lake. There are camping facilities, picnic areas, a playground, swimming, fishing, ramp for boating and rental boats. For more information, call (318) 766-3530.

VILLE PLATTE

Chicot State Park, 8 miles north of Ville Platte, off SR 319, consists of 6,400 acres of woodlands with a lake. There are camping facilities, picnic areas, hiking trails, a boat ramp for boating, fishing, a swimming pool and nature programs. For more information, call (318) 363-2403.

WESTWEGO

Bayou Segnette State Park, off US 90, consists of 580 acres of woodlands and marsh areas with camping facilities, picnic areas, hiking trails, a boat ramp, fishing and swimming. For more information, call (504) 736-7140 or 736-7145.

ZWOLLE

North Toledo Bend State Park, located 4 miles southwest of Zwolle off Highway 3229, has 990 acres. The park features camping, picnic areas, a playground, hiking trails, a ramp for boating, fishing, a swimming pool and a visitors' center. For more information, call (318) 645-4715.

Mississippi

PETS WELCOME!
Mississippi

Comfort Inn on the Hill

Comfort Inn on the Hill
6595 US Highway 49 North
Hattiesburg, MS 39402
800-228-5150 ▪ (601) 268-2170

Room Rates:	$54–$100, including deluxe continental breakfast. AAA and AARP discounts.
Pet Charges or Deposits:	None. Small pets up to 25 lbs.
Rated: 3 Paws 🐾🐾🐾	118 comfortable rooms with refrigerators, microwaves, cable television, in-room movies, laundry facilities, swimming pool, exercise room, restaurant and lounge.

Set in the beautiful, rolling hills of the Mississippi Pine Belt is the charming town of Hattiesburg, recently voted "America's most livable small city." Here you will find the Comfort Inn on the Hill, where the central location provides easy access to area attractions, the Mississippi Gulf Coast, Jackson, Mobile and New Orleans.

A complimentary deluxe continental breakfast in the Summit Restaurant is included in your room rate. The inn features an exercise room and swimming pool.

Crowne Plaza Hotel

Crowne Plaza Hotel
200 East Amite Street
Jackson, MS 39201
(601) 969-5100

Room Rates:	$59–$89. AAA and AARP discounts.
Pet Charges or Deposits:	$25 per stay, plus $100 refundable deposit. Manager's approval required.
Rated: 3 Paws 🐾🐾🐾	354 guest rooms with office-sized desk area, pay-per-view movies, irons and ironing boards, video-express checkout, some wet bars, microwaves, refrigerators, exercise room, pool, laundry facilities, restaurant and cocktail lounge.

The Crowne Plaza Hotel towers over the heart of metropolitan Jackson. This 23-story luxury hotel and convention center caters to business travelers and families on vacation. You will enjoy the personal, friendly service traditionally associated with Crowne Plaza Hotels, with the added benefit of Southern hospitality.

In addition to elegantly appointed rooms, guest amenities include a corporate floor with a fitness center, a swimming pool, a gift shop for those little extras you might need, plus a panoramic view of the city.

For your dining pleasure, the Bristol Bar and Grill offers the freshest ingredients with varied breakfast, lunch and dinner menus. Breakfast features traditional favorites. A luncheon buffet features specialty salads, fresh fruits, homemade soups and breads, as well as prepared-to-order sandwiches, burgers and daily specials. The dinner menu offers an assortment of entrées to suit any palate.

Residence Inn by Marriott

Residence Inn by Marriott
881 East River Place
Jackson, MS 39202
800-331-3131 ▪ (601) 355-3599

Room Rates:	$109–$149, including continental breakfast. AAA and AARP discounts.
Pet Charges or Deposits:	$75–$95 cleaning fee.
Rated: 3 Paws 🐾🐾🐾	120 luxury suites with separate living room, fully equipped kitchen, fireplace, laundry facilities, barbecue facilities, outdoor pool, two hot tubs, complimentary breakfast buffet, social hour and grocery shopping service.

When you have to be away on business or you are on vacation with your family, the Residence Inn by Marriott gives you that home-away-from-home feeling. The inn's comforts and conveniences, spacious suites with separate sleeping and living areas, fully equipped kitchens, daily maid service, grocery shopping service, laundry facilities, work areas and meeting facilities, as well as the manager-hosted continental breakfast buffet and informal hospitality hour, all add up to make your accommodations more like a home than a hotel. Upon check-in, pets receive complimentary pet dishes for their food and water, plus a special room magnet for the room door to let housekeeping know you have a pet with you.

This restful retreat offers a heated swimming pool, two hot tubs and a barbecue area. The beautifully landscaped grounds and walking path are perfect for morning or evening strolls with pets.

Oliver-Britt House Inn

Oliver-Britt House Inn
512 Van Buren Avenue
Oxford, MS 38655
(601) 234-8043

Room Rates:	$45–$65, including full breakfast on weekends. AAA, AARP, AKC and ABA discounts.
Pet Charges or Deposits:	None.
Rated: 4 Paws 😺 😺 😺 😺	5 guest rooms furnished with antiques and reproductions, with private baths, cable television, central heat and air.

T he Oliver-Britt House Inn is only a short walk from the University of Mississippi campus and only minutes away from Rowan Oak, the home of William Faulkner, and from historical Oxford Square.

The restored manor house offers five spacious guest rooms, uniquely decorated with period antiques and reproductions, with queen- or king-sized beds, private baths, cable television and central heating and air conditioning.

On the weekends, guests are treated to a full Southern-style breakfast before they start their day of sightseeing or business meetings. The innkeepers, Glynn Oliver and Mary Ann Britt, are there to assist you with your travel needs. They will help you plan your business trip or vacation to the Oxford area.

La Font Inn – Resort and Conference Center

La Font Inn – Resort and Conference Center
Highway 90 East
Pascagoula, MS 35968
800-647-6077 ▪ (601) 762-7111

Room Rates: $55–$69. AAA and AARP discounts.
Pet Charges or Deposits: None
Rated: 5 Paws 🐾🐾🐾🐾🐾   192 guest rooms. Olympic-sized swimming pool, heated whirlpool, playground, shuffleboard, indoor sauna, exercise and weight room, restaurant and cocktail lounge.

Set amid nine beautifully landscaped acres, the La Font Inn—Resort and Conference Center offers such amenities as refrigerators stocked with purified water, wet bars, kitchenettes, steam baths, recliners and sofas, large dining-work areas, in-room coffee and cable television.

Guests may spend their day relaxing by the Olympic-sized swimming pool, soaking in the heated whirlpool, working out in the exercise and weight room, relaxing in the indoor sauna or playing a game or two of shuffleboard or tennis. For younger guests, there is a playground to enjoy. Four-legged guests will no doubt love exploring the nine acres of landscaped property.

Cottage Inn

Cottage Inn
4325 Casino Center Drive
Robinsonville, MS 38664
800-363-2985 ▪ (601) 363-2900

Room Rates:	$65–$175, including continental breakfast.
Pet Charges or Deposits:	None. Limit 3 pets.
Rated: 4 Paws 🐾🐾🐾🐾	9 cottage chalets, 1 Presidential Suite with Jacuzzi; all rooms are beautifully furnished and include refrigerators, microwaves, some fireplaces and air conditioning.

L ocated in Robinsonville, minutes from the Casino Center of Mississippi, is the Cottage Inn. Here, guests will find charming cottage chalets, each with two spacious and elegantly furnished rooms.

There are four types of cottages from which to choose, with accommodations that offer fireplaces, living rooms and full kitchens, all with separate sleeping quarters and vaulted ceilings. The 2,500-square-foot Presidential Suite is great for honeymooners, families or those looking for more spacious accommodations. The living area features a fireplace, a full kitchen and a sofa bed for additional guests, plus a Jacuzzi for two.

The spacious 5-acre grounds are perfect for a walk with your dog before you head out for a day of sightseeing or a visit to one of the local casinos.

The Corners Bed and Breakfast Inn

The Corners Bed and Breakfast Inn
601 Klein Street
Vicksburg, MS 39180
800-444-7421 ▪ (601) 636-7421

Room Rates: $85–$120, including full breakfast. AAA discounts.
Pet Charges or Deposits: None.
Rated: 4 Paws 🐾🐾🐾🐾   13 guest rooms and 1 luxury suite, all with private baths,
                                              whirlpool tubs, furnished with antiques, canopy beds,
                                              fireplaces, private terraces, refrigerators and microwaves.

Built in 1873, The Corners Bed and Breakfast Inn beckons guests to take a step back in time amid Victorian elegance and country simplicity. The inn's pierced columns and parterre gardens have earned its registry to the National Register of Historic Places.

Fifteen beautifully appointed guest rooms provide a variety of memorable experiences. Stay in rooms with true Southern elegance or Victorian charm or country simplicity. All are furnished in antiques and have private baths. Choose from canopied beds, fireplaces, whirlpool tubs, private porches and views.

The inn is perched atop a bluff overlooking the Mississippi Valley, with the Mississippi River off in the distance, so you will want to spend some quiet time taking in the magnificent sunsets from your rocker on your private porch or on the 68-foot front gallery porch.

Duff Green Mansion Inn

Duff Green Mansion Inn
1114 First East Street
Vicksburg, MS 39180
800-992-0037 ▪ (601) 636-6968 or 638-6662

Room Rates: $75–$160, including full breakfast.
Pet Charges or Deposits: None. Small pets only. Manager's approval required.
Rated: 4 Paws 🐾🐾🐾🐾   4 guest rooms and 3 suites, National Register mansion,
                                          swimming pool.

T he Duff Green Mansion Inn in Vicksburg's historical district is considered one of the finest examples of Palladian architecture in the state of Mississippi. The property was originally a wedding gift to Mary Lake Green from her parents, Judge and Mrs. William Lake Green.

Built for his bride in 1856 by the prosperous merchant, Duff Green, the antebellum mansion was the center for many parties and celebrations. When the Confederate and Union soldiers battled in Vicksburg, the estate was shelled, but managed to survive and was quickly converted to a hospital, which it remained until the end of the war.

This 12,000-square-foot mansion has been restored and contains seven guest rooms offering delightful accommodations, antique furnishings of the period and hearty Southern breakfasts. There is plenty of room on the grounds and in several local parks for you and your dog to explore.

WHERE TO TAKE YOUR PET IN
Mississippi

Please Note: *Pets must be on a leash at all times and may be restricted to certain areas. For directions, use fees, pet charges and general information, contact the numbers listed below.*

National Forest and Seashore

FOREST

Bienville National Forest encompasses 179,402 acres of pine and hardwood forests in central Mississippi. Visitors will find camping, picnic areas, hiking and horse trails, a boat ramp for boating, boat rentals, fishing, swimming and a visitors' center. For more information, call (601) 469-3811.

OCEAN SPRINGS

Gulf Islands National Seashore, in southern Mississippi, is a 135,000-acre recreation area east of Ocean Springs in the Davis Bayou area. Visitors will find camping, picnic areas, a boat ramp for boating, fishing, swimming, nature programs and a visitors' center. For more information, call (601) 875-9057.

Army Corps of Engineers

BATESVILLE

Enid Lake, located 12 miles south of Batesville on I-55, is a 15,500-acre lake with camping, picnic areas, hiking and bicycle trails, a boat ramp for boating, fishing and swimming. For more information, call (601) 563-4571.

GRENADA

Grenada Lake, located 3 miles northeast of Grenada, encompasses 35,820 acres and offers camping, picnic areas, hiking trails, a boat ramp for boating, boat rentals, fishing, swimming, nature programs and a visitors' center. For more information, call (601) 226-5911.

SARDIS

Sardis Lake and Dam, located 5 miles east of Sardis off I-55, has 32,100-acre recreational area offering camping, picnic areas, hiking trails, a boat ramp for boating, boat rentals, fishing and swimming. Call (601) 563-4531 for more information.

State Parks

COLUMBUS

Lake Lowndes State Park, located 6 miles southeast of Columbus off SR 69, has 750 acres with camping, picnic areas, hiking trails, tennis, a boat ramp for boating, boat rentals, fishing, swimming, a nature center and a visitors' center. For more information, call (601) 328-2110.

GRENADA

Hugh White State Park, located 5 miles east of Grenada off SR 8, encompasses 1,256 acres of parkland with camping, picnic areas, hiking trails, tennis, a boat ramp for boating, boat rentals, fishing, swimming, water skiing, a nature program and a visitors' center. For more information, call (601) 226-4934.

HOLLANDALE

Leroy Percy State Park, located 6 miles west of Hollandale on SR 12, consists of 2,371 acres of parkland with camping, picnic areas, hiking trails, boating, boat rentals, fishing, swimming, a nature program and a visitors' center. For more information, call (601) 827-5436.

JACKSON

LeFleur's Bluff State Park, off I-55 North at East Lakeland, exit in Jackson, consists of 310 acres with camping, picnic areas, hiking trails, golf, tennis, playground, a boat ramp for boating, boat rentals, fishing, swimming and a visitors' center. For more information, call (601) 987-3923.

McCOMB

Percy Quin State Park, located 5 miles southwest of McComb off I-55, is a 1,700-acre park with camping, picnic areas, hiking trails, a boat ramp for boating, boat rentals, fishing, swimming, water skiing, a nature program and a visitors' center. For more information, call (601) 684-3938.

NATCHEZ

Natchez State Park, 10 miles north of Natchez off US 61, is a 3,411-acre park with camping, picnic areas, nature and hiking trails, a boat ramp, boat rentals, fishing and a visitors' center. For more information, call (601) 442-2658.

OAKLAND

George Payne Cossar State Park, located 5 miles northeast of Oakland on SR 32, near Batesville, is a 982-acre park offering camping, picnic areas, hiking trails, a boat ramp for boating, boat rentals, water skiing, fishing, swimming and a visitors' center. For more information, call (601) 623-7356.

PONTOTOC

Trace State Park, 10 miles east of Pontotoc off SR 6, near Tupelo, encompasses 1,980 acres of parkland with camping, picnic areas, hiking and bicycle trails, a boat ramp for boating, boat rentals, fishing, swimming and a visitors' center. For more information, call (601) 489-2958.

QUITMAN

Clarkco State Park, located 5 miles north of Quitman on US 45, has 815 acres of parkland. Visitors will find camping, picnic areas, hiking trails, a boat ramp for boating, boat rentals, fishing, swimming and a visitors' center. For more information, call (601) 776-6651.

ROSEDALE

Great River Road State Park, off SR 1 near Rosedale, consists of 731 acres of parkland offering camping, picnic areas, hiking trails, a boat ramp for boating, boat rentals, fishing and a visitors' center. Call (601) 759-6762 for more information.

SARDIS

John W. Kyle State Park, 9 miles east of Sardis on SR 315, with 740 acres of parkland with camping, picnic areas, hiking trails, tennis, a boat ramp for boating, boat rentals, fishing, swimming, water skiing, a nature program and a visitors' center. For more information, call (601) 487-1683.

TISHOMINGO

Tishomingo State Park, located 2 miles east of Tishomingo off SR 25, encompasses 1,340 acres of parkland with camping, picnic areas, hiking trails, a boat ramp for boating, boat rentals, fishing, swimming, a nature program and a visitors' center. For more information, call (601) 438-6914.

WAVELAND

Buccaneer State Park, located off US 90 at Waveland, near Bay St. Louis, encompasses 398 acres of parkland offering camping, picnic areas, hiking trails, fishing, swimming and a visitors' center. Call (601) 467-3822 for more information.

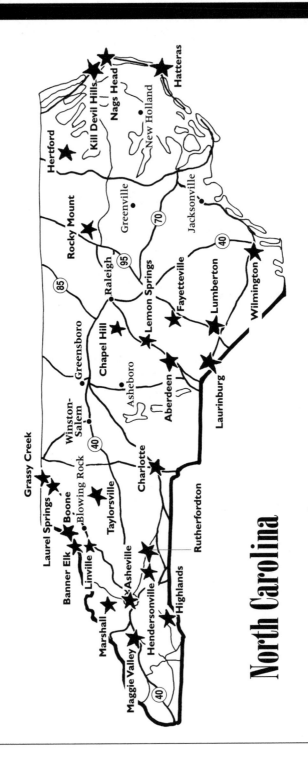

North Carolina

PETS WELCOME!

North Carolina

Inn at the Bryant House

Inn at the Bryant House
214 North Poplar Street
Aberdeen, NC 28315
800-453-4019 ▪ (910) 944-3300

Room Rates:	$50–$85, including continental breakfast.
Pet Charges or Deposits:	None.
Rated: 4 Paws 🐾🐾🐾🐾	9 rooms and 2 luxury suites, twin to king-sized beds, most with private baths, antique furnishings, cable television, non-smoking inn.

Built in 1913, the Inn at the Bryant House is a turn-of-the-century home that has been completely restored and converted into a charming bed and breakfast inn. The inn has maintained its Southern splendor of the past, while adding modern conveniences of today.

Welcoming and tranquil pastel colors flow through the entire house. The spacious common rooms offer a friendly, relaxed atmosphere, inviting guests to gather around the fire or relax on the front porch. Guests are invited to enjoy a delicious continental breakfast, served in the dining room or garden room, featuring fresh-baked breads, homemade jams, jellies and preserves, and a wide selection of cereals, homemade granola, seasonal fruits and piping hot coffee or tea. Plus, the resident dog will be glad to show you and your pet some four-legged Southern hospitality.

This non-smoking inn is located in the downtown historic district, set amid the rolling North Carolina hills, close to many regional points of interest such as historical sites, nature preserves, polo and equestrian clubs and more than 30 golf courses.

Comfort Inn – River Ridge

Comfort Inn – River Ridge
800 Fairview Road
Asheville, NC 28803
800-836-6732 ▪ (704) 298-9141

Room Rates:	$49–$159, including deluxe continental breakfast. AAA and AARP discounts.
Pet Charges or Deposits:	None.
Rated: 3 Paws ❀ ❀ ❀	154 guest rooms and 24 luxury suites with in-room coffee makers, cable television, in-room movies; outdoor hot tub, swimming pool, playground area, basketball and volleyball courts, horseshoes, jogging and walking area, decks, grills and picnic tables.

The Comfort Inn – River Ridge is located on 35 acres of rolling hills surrounded by the Great Smoky Mountains. Spacious accommodations include coffee makers, cable television, in-room movies, private balconies with mountain views, separate living rooms, kitchenettes, wet bars, microwaves and Jacuzzi tubs.

The complimentary continental breakfast, served in the large sitting room complete with fireplace and television, is a great way to start your day. For your recreational needs, the inn has an outdoor swimming pool, basketball and volleyball courts, horseshoes, jogging and walking area, plus a playground area for the younger guests. For those who wish to spend the afternoon relaxing, there is an outdoor hot tub overlooking the Smoky Mountains, to soak your cares away. Or light up the outdoor grill and have a private picnic. Plus, with acres of hillside, there is plenty of room for you and your dog to stretch your legs.

Dogwood Cottage Inn

Dogwood Cottage Inn
40 Canterbury Road, North
Asheville, NC 28801-1560
(704) 258-9725

Room Rates:	$95–$105, including full breakfast.
Pet Charges or Deposits:	Call for deposit.
Rated: 4 Paws 🐾🐾🐾🐾	4 rooms with private baths, large sitting areas, shared balcony, heated pool, large country porch.

Built in the late 1890s, the Dogwood Cottage Inn offers guests 7,000 square feet of Appalachian, rustic, shingle-style architecture. Originally named The Manor, it was built by a visitor to the area, Mr. Raoul, who found it difficult to book hotel rooms for his family of five children and servants. Twenty other similar "cottages" were erected in the area for the same reason. The Manor served as the focal point for most social events for cottage guests.

Now the rustic cottage has been transformed into a quaint bed and breakfast inn. From the 42-foot veranda and the polished hardwood floors to the oak-beamed ceilings and large fireplace in the parlor, the Dogwood Cottage is a charming hideaway and yet is less than 2 miles from downtown Asheville.

Guests may choose from the Colonial Blue Room with French doors looking out onto the pool; the English Country Garden Room, decorated in bounteous flower prints; the Americana Red Room, decorated in Early American, including quilts and rugs; or the Forest Green Room with its rich tones of forest green and gold. All rooms have queen-sized beds, private baths and lots of charm. The spacious grounds and area attractions will beckon you and your dog to explore them.

Banner Elk Inn Bed and Breakfast

Banner Elk Inn Bed and Breakfast
Route 3, Box 1134
Banner Elk, NC 28604
800-972-2183 ▪ (704) 898-6223

Room Rates:	$80–$150, including full breakfast.
Pet Charges or Deposits:	Call for fees and deposits. Manager's approval required.
Rated: 4 Paws 🐾🐾🐾🐾	3 guest rooms and 1 large suite, all with down comforters, Victorian or French provincial decor, 3 with private baths.

When looking for a quiet, cozy bed and breakfast inn that welcomes both you and your pet, look no further than the Banner Elk Inn Bed and Breakfast. Once a country church, this 1912 inn is located near Mount Pisgah National Park, great for summer fun or winter skiing. It has been renovated and furnished with antiques collected from around the world.

The five lovely rooms offer guests soft, restful hues and Victorian or French provincial decor. Lin's Peach Room has a majestic wooden Victorian queen-sized bed and full private bath. Jeanne's Mauve Room offers a romantic Victorian motif with an antique brass bed and full bath. Jeannie and Linda's Room is colorfully decorated with stripes, bright colors and pewter twin beds. For a French provincial suite that sleeps up to four, Bonnie's Blue Room is a wonderful choice.

No matter which room you choose, you will enjoy the European down comforters, Southern hospitality and a full breakfast of homemade breads, fresh fruit and a variety of special dishes.

Grandma Jean's Bed and Breakfast

Grandma Jean's Bed and Breakfast
254 Meadow View Drive
Boone, NC 28607
(704) 262-3670

Room Rates:	$65–$75, including continental breakfast.
Pet Charges or Deposits:	Call for charges. Small pets only. Please bring carrier. Manager's approval required.
Rated: 3 Paws 🐾🐾🐾	4 attractive rooms, shared baths and large front porch.

At Grandma Jean's Bed and Breakfast, they have their own way of looking at things. Grandma Jean says, "No antiques. Not a restored mansion. Plain rooms, but friendly." You won't find anything fancy here, just good old Southern hospitality. Everything runs at a slower pace, reflecting the nostalgic past.

Built in 1920, this charming two-story country home is within minutes of most scenic attractions. Grandma aims for 100 percent guest satisfaction, with most guests vowing to return. This is the perfect place for busy people to lose themselves in Southern grace and hospitality. Relax under a shade tree with the dog, or roam around the rambling yard and country garden. There is even a porch swing and hammock to while away the day. If you like, Grandma Jean will join you for that second cup of coffee on the front porch.

Carolina Mornings Inc.

Carolina Mornings Inc.
109 Circadian Way
Chapel Hill, NC 27516
888-667-6467 ▪ (919) 929-5553

Room Rates:	$85 and up per night. Weekly rates available.
Pet Charges or Deposits:	Call for fees and deposits. Manager's approval required.
Rated: 4 Paws 🐾🐾🐾🐾	6 cabins for 2 to 6 people each with fully equipped kitchens, full baths, telephones, cable television, large porches or decks, some with fireplaces and laundry facilities.

When looking for a relaxing, private retreat for your next vacation or weekend getaway, Carolina Mornings Inc.'s reservation service will help you find the perfect place. Choose from The Sugar Creek Studio, Cabin on Eagles Nest, Little House in Hot Springs, Sunny Acres Farm, Dream Wanderer or Dun Romin'.

These cabins are all set in the woods, some near ponds, creeks or mountain streams. Though the accommodations vary by the cabin you choose, most will sleep from two to six people, have fully equipped kitchens, full baths, cable televisions and VCRs, laundry facilities, fireplaces, outdoor grills, covered porches or large decks.

Centrally located near many local attractions and Great Smoky Mountains National Park, there's always plenty to keep you busy. Spend the day with your dog exploring the mountain trails, picnic near a stream, try your hand at fishing or relax with a glass of wine and a good book on your private porch or deck.

Hilton at University Place

Hilton at University Place
8629 J.M. Keynes Drive
Charlotte, NC 28262
(704) 547-7444

Room Rates:	$89–$159
Pet Charges or Deposits:	$50 per stay. Dogs up to 25 lbs. No cats, please.
Rated: 3 Paws 🐾🐾🐾	243 guest rooms and 3 suites, in-room coffee makers, some with microwaves and refrigerators, cable television, in-room movies, swimming pool, fitness center, volleyball court, valet laundry, small lake with seasonal paddleboats, restaurant and cocktail lounge.

C onveniently located in the fast-paced metropolis of Charlotte is the Hilton at University Place, the centerpiece of the University Place complex of unique shops and fashionable restaurants.

The guest rooms here are large and comfortable and many rooms have dramatic views of Lake Norman. Hilton amenities include remote-control televisions, data ports, in-room movies, valet laundry service, microwaves, refrigerators and a well-equipped fitness center and outdoor pool.

Dining at the Upper Deck Grill, one of North Charlotte's most noted restaurants, offers an eclectic menu blending Southern, Tex-Mex and Oriental cuisine. The Upper Deck Beach Club is a popular nightspot.

Holiday Inn – Bordeaux

Holiday Inn – Bordeaux
1707 Owen Drive
Fayetteville, NC 28304
800-325-0211 ▪ (910) 323-0111

Room Rates:	$59–$85. AAA and AARP discounts.
Pet Charges or Deposits:	$100 refundable deposit, plus a signed agreement or credit card imprint.
Rated: 3 Paws 🐾🐾🐾	289 guest rooms and 7 luxury suites with in-room coffee, cable television, in-room movies, some refrigerators, swimming pool, exercise room, valet laundry, airport transportation, restaurant and cocktail lounge.

The Holiday Inn – Bordeaux prides itself on friendly service with amenities that make you feel right at home. Accommodations include in-room coffee, cable television, in-room movies, plus some rooms with refrigerators. For added luxury, choose the concierge floor, which offers an extra touch of class with king-sized executive rooms, a complimentary breakfast and evening hors d'oeuvres. If you wish, you may start your day with a workout at the hotel's Bordeaux Fitness Connection, followed by a refreshing dip in the swimming pool. Pets will appreciate the special exercise area set aside just for them. The Game Room is a great place to test your skill at darts, pool, foos ball, golf putting or relaxing with your favorite spirits and watching the game on the big-screen television.

For your dining pleasure, the Café Bordeaux serves breakfast, lunch and dinner in a casual atmosphere. Top off your day with an evening at Bowties, one of Fayetteville's favorite night spots for live entertainment.

River House Inn and Restaurant

River House Inn and Restaurant
1896 Old Field Creek Road
Grassy Creek, NC 28631
(910) 982-2109

Room Rates: $90–$170, including full breakfast.
Pet Charges or Deposits: 1 night's room rate as deposit.
Rated: 4 Paws ❀❀❀❀ 6 spacious guest rooms with king- or queen-sized beds,
          private bathrooms, whirlpool hot tubs, decorated with
          antiques, private porches with river or mountain views,
          restaurant.

Perched on 125 acres on the banks of the North Fork River is the enchanting River House Inn and Restaurant. This country inn consists of six charming guest rooms decorated with antiques and featuring private baths and inviting private porches with breathtaking views of the river or mountains.

Spend the day relaxing in a rocking chair on the porch, picnic under the giant sycamore trees down by the river or head out for a day of hiking and exploration. If you are feeling truly adventurous, you can rent canoes, go horseback riding or visit the Grayson Highlands State Park, the Creeper Trail or one of the many other local sites. Once you have worked up an appetite, a sumptuous dinner awaits you at the River House Restaurant.

Hatteras Cabañas and Cottages

Hatteras Cabañas and Cottages
PO Box 387
Hatteras, NC 27943
800-338-4775 ▪ (919) 986-2241

Room Rates:	$51–$70
Pet Charges or Deposits:	$40 per stay.
Rated: 3 Paws 🐾🐾🐾	40 cabañas, cottages and condos, with a variety of amenities ranging from twin or trundle beds to queen-sized beds, decks, efficiency kitchens, cable television, central air and heat.

O n the oceanfront at Cape Hatteras National Seashore you'll find Hatteras Cabañas and Cottages. These shoreline cabañas, cottages and condos offer visitors a relaxing home away from home where you can bring the entire family, including the pets.

Your efficiency accommodations feature twin beds, trundle beds or queen-sized beds, high decks to enjoy the breathtaking view or relax in the sun, efficiency kitchens to make mealtimes easier, central air and heating for your comfort any time of the year and sleeping accommodations for two to four guests. Spend your day relaxing on the deck, exploring the beachfront or fishing at one of the many great recreational areas.

Quality Inn and Suites

Quality Inn and Suites
201 Sugar Loaf Road
Hendersonville, NC 28792
800-228-5151 • (704) 692-7231

Room Rates:	$45–$140, including continental breakfast. AAA and AARP discounts.
Pet Charges or Deposits:	Call for deposit. Small pets only.
Rated: 3 Paws 🐾🐾🐾	149 guest rooms and 16 spacious suites with cable television, free movies, some rooms with in-room coffee makers, microwaves, refrigerators, Jacuzzis, plus indoor swimming pool, sauna, whirlpool/Jacuzzi, fitness room, game room, free airport transportation, restaurant and cocktail lounge.

Quality Inn and Suites is located in the green mountains of western North Carolina. This full-service hotel offers guests Southern hospitality with large, comfortable guest rooms chock-full with amenities.

Start your day off with the complimentary continental breakfast before heading out for a day of sightseeing in this historical area. The Blue Ridge Parkway is the perfect place to take your pet. This 469-mile scenic road connects the Shenandoah National Park in Virginia and the Great Smoky Mountains National Park in North Carolina and Tennessee, and includes five different parks where pets are welcome.

Recreational activities in the area are abundant. You may go hiking, white-water rafting, horseback riding, stream fishing, golfing or relax with a picnic under a shady tree. If you wish to stay close to the hotel, there is the fitness room for an invigorating workout, the indoor heated pool for a refreshing swim, the game room to keep kids of all ages happy, and the mini putt-putt to practice your putting.

Beechtree Inn

Beechtree Inn
Route 1, Box 517
Hertford, NC 27944
(919) 426-7815

Room Rates:	$45–$80, including full breakfast.
Pet Charges or Deposits:	Call for deposit. Manager's approval required.
Rated: 4 Paws 🐾🐾🐾🐾	3 guest houses with period antiques, full bathrooms, some with fireplaces, wooded surroundings. Furniture-making classes available.

If you are looking for accommodations with true Southern heritage, the Beechtree Inn fits the bill. Over the last 20 years the Hobbs family has assembled a collection of 14 pre-Civil War buildings, restored them and furnished them with a collection of period antiques and fine reproductions made by Benjamin C. Hobbs, an experienced furniture maker. Three of these buildings have been restored and turned into delightful guest accommodations.

The Bennetts Creek House, built in 1750, offers a queen-sized bed and loft, while the Pratt Wing boasts a queen-sized bed and full bath. The Bear Swamp House, which welcomes pets, was built in 1837. The house has the original woodwork and working fireplace, a large bedroom with queen-sized bed, a sitting room with sofa bed and television, and a full bath.

The wooded grounds surrounding each building are perfect for an afternoon stroll with your dog. There are plenty of local attractions to keep you entertained. Plus, an extra attraction is a week-long furniture-making class with Mr. Hobbs, which allows you to take home a piece of furniture you made with your own two hands.

Fire Mountain Inn and Cabins

Fire Mountain Inn and Cabins
PO Box 2772
Highlands, NC 28741
800-775-4446 ▪ (704) 526-4446

Room Rates: $85–$175, including continental breakfast.
Pet Charges or Deposits: $10 per day; $150 deposit. Dogs under 30 lbs. No cats, please.
Rated: 5 Paws ❖❖❖❖❖   6 inn rooms, 3 suites and 6 cabins. Amenities include wood-
                         burning stone fireplaces, private terraces, kitchenettes and full
                         kitchens, Jacuzzi tubs, television, VCR, and spectacular views.

Fire Mountain Inn and Cabins are built atop a mountain with uninter-rupted, dramatic views. This modern inn is ideal for people who want to bask in the best that Mother Nature has to offer while enjoying the ultimate in sophistication and comfort. Inspired by the beauty of Fire Mountain, this resplendent inn is a private world unto itself. Spectacular views abound from every room and suite. The cabins offer guests full kitchens, native stone fireplaces, vaulted ceilings and plenty of privacy. Each room and cabin opens to a large deck or terrace, perfect for lounging in the mountain splendor, snoozing in the healthy mountain air or taking in the most breathtaking sun-rises and sunsets one could imagine.

After you have feasted on the continental breakfast, head out for a day of adventure. There are four hiking trails with ponds, streams and waterfalls, plus Great Smoky Mountains National Park for you and your dog to explore.

Ramada Inn

Ramada Inn
1701 South Virginia Dare Trail
Kill Devil Hills, NC 27948
800-635-1824 ▪ (919) 441-2151

Room Rates:	$69–$172
Pet Charges or Deposits:	$10 per stay.
Rated: 3 Paws 🐾🐾🐾	172 guest rooms with coffee makers, microwaves, refrigerators, cable television, in-room movies, private balconies, many with ocean views, heated indoor swimming pool, whirlpool, shuffleboard, volleyball, restaurant and cocktail lounge. Kennels on site.

S et on the Outer Banks of the scenic Nags Head Beach is the oceanfront Ramada Inn. Tastefully decorated, accommodations include in-room coffee makers, microwaves, refrigerators and cable television. All rooms have private balconies, many with breathtaking views of the beach. Relax and unwind in the hotel whirlpool, swim a few laps in the indoor heated swimming pool or visit the quaint fishing villages, beautiful gardens and lighthouses in the area.

You and your dog may wish to wander down to the beach for a relaxing stroll or a chance to soak up some sun. There are lots of exciting places to see and things to do year round in Kill Devil Hills. Winter at Nags Head Beach is ideal for shell collecting. Spring is a fisherman's paradise. Fall offers the warmest temperatures and is considered the best season by the locals. In the summer, soak up the sunshine at the hotel's Gazebo Deck Bar, where you can enjoy your favorite spirits.

Doughton-Hall Bed and Breakfast Inn

Doughton-Hall Bed and Breakfast Inn
12668 North Carolina Highway 18 South
Laurel Springs, NC 28644
800-484-1170 ▪ (910) 359-2341

Room Rates:	$80, including full breakfast and evening wine and hors d'oeuvres.
Pet Charges or Deposits:	None.
Rated: 3 Paws ❧❧❧	4 guest rooms with double and queen-sized beds, 3 private baths, large hot tub, trout stream on property.

L ocated near the Blue Ridge Parkway, a 469-mile scenic road connecting the Shenandoah National Park in Virginia and the Great Smoky Mountains National Park in North Carolina and Tennessee, is the historic Doughton-Hall Bed and Breakfast Inn. Built in the 1890s for former Congressman Robert L. Doughton, this cozy Queen Anne-style inn offers four guest rooms with double or queen-sized beds, three with private baths.

The inn hosts love to spoil their guests, starting with a sumptuous traditional country buffet breakfast of country ham, eggs, grits, fluffy soufflés and croissants. After a large breakfast, you may want to relax with a second cup of coffee on the front porch and listen to the rushing water of the creek in front of the inn, relax in the hot tub or venture on down to the pond or gazebo. For anglers, the creek is perfect for trout fishing. When dinner rolls around, there are several exceptional restaurants in town where you can dine with the local folks, or your hosts will prepare a special private dinner for you with advance notice.

Hampton Inn of Laurinburg

Hampton Inn of Laurinburg
115 Hampton Court
Laurinburg, NC 28352
800-HAMPTON ▪ (910) 277-1516

Room Rates: $58–$80, including continental breakfast.
Pet Charges or Deposits: None. Manager's approval required.
Rated: 3 Paws 🐾🐾🐾   50 guest rooms with color televisions, free in-room movies,
                                    refrigerators, microwaves, swimming pool, valet service,
                                    complimentary newspaper, walking distance to restaurants and
                                    shops.

Conveniently located in the heart of Laurinburg, within walking distance of shopping, restaurants and St. Andrews College, is the Hampton Inn. Your accommodations will include a complimentary deluxe continental breakfast, free movie channels and other cable networks, valet service, complimentary daily newspaper, coffee and fruit available for guests 24 hours a day, plus a complimentary social hour on Tuesday and Thursday evenings.

Spend your day poolside, strolling the spacious grounds with your dog, or visiting one of the many historic sites and recreational parks in the surrounding areas.

Whispering Winds Bed and Breakfast

Whispering Winds Bed and Breakfast
4700 Laws Road
Lemon Springs, NC 28355
(919) 774-7036

Room Rates:	$65, including full breakfast.
Pet Charges or Deposits:	$5 per day. Manager's approval and proof of vaccinations required. No cats, please.
Rated: 3 Paws 🐾🐾🐾	2 rooms with turn-of-the-century antiques and scenic views of the surrounding wooded area, fireplace in common living room, outdoor hot tub, exercise area and kennels.

L ocated only minutes from Raleigh and Fayetteville, the Whispering Winds Bed and Breakfast offers guests comfortable accommodations in a homey, wooded setting. Guests may enjoy a generous breakfast that includes herbs and fruits from the garden, and menus featuring low-fat, low-cholesterol foods. You may wish to spend your day hiking with the dog or grab your mountain bike and explore the surrounding trails.

If relaxation is more your speed, then curl up with a good book and a glass of wine in front of a roaring fire in the cozy living room or soak your cares away in the hot tub tucked beneath the Carolina pines. If you wish, you can play a friendly game of horseshoes, or go fishing in the nearby pond. Maybe you'll catch dinner!

Linville Cottage Inn

Linville Cottage Inn
PO Box 508
Linville, NC 28646
(704) 733-6551

Room Rates:	$65–$95, including full breakfast.
Pet Charges or Deposits:	Call for deposit. Small pets only. Manager's approval required.
Rated: 3 Paws ❧❧❧	4 rooms decorated with English country antiques. Dog runs and exercise areas.

The high country of North Carolina is home to the charming Linville Cottage Inn. This delightful country inn offers guests affordable accommodations, with guest rooms furnished with country antiques and collectibles.

Take a stroll with your dog around the grounds and inhale the scents of the aromatic herb gardens that surround the inn to work up an appetite for your full continental breakfast of homemade breads and baked goods, with fresh jellies, jams and preserves from the bounty of the garden.

There are endless activities located within a short distance of the inn, such as fishing, hiking, whitewater rafting, canoeing, skiing and mountain climbing. For truly inspirational views, try the hiking trails with a mile-high swinging bridge at Grandfather Mountain.

Comfort Suites

Comfort Suites
215 Wintergreen Drive
Lumberton, NC 28358
800-964-7700 ▪ (910) 739-8800

Room Rates:	$60–$100, including continental breakfast and manager's reception. AAA and AARP discounts.
Pet Charges or Deposits:	$50 refundable deposit.
Rated: 3 Paws 🐾🐾🐾	93 one-bedroom suites with sitting areas, refrigerators, microwaves, coffee makers, VCRs, outdoor pool, fitness room, sauna, valet dry cleaning and Jacuzzi suites.

L ocated on the Lumberton River is the historic town of Lumberton, founded by a Revolutionary War officer, Captain John Willis. It is also the home of the Comfort Suites. This comfortable, affordable inn offers one-bedroom suites with sitting areas, refrigerators, microwaves, coffee makers, color television sets and VCRs, perfect for a business trip or a family vacation. There are also suites with private Jacuzzis available.

Guests may use the outdoor pool, the fitness room and the sauna. Make sure to take advantage of the manager's reception during the week. The central location of Comfort Suites makes it easy to reach the historic cities of Fayetteville and Wilmington, both near the Cape Fear River, where you can take in all of the historic sites.

Country Cabins

Country Cabins
171 Bradley Street
Maggie Valley, NC 28751
888-222-4611 • (704) 926-0612

Room Rates:	$65–$110
Pet Charges or Deposits:	$1 per pound, per stay. Manager's approval required.
Rated: 4 Paws 🐾🐾🐾🐾	5 log cabins with full kitchens or kitchenettes, private baths, fireplaces, color televisions and covered porches with rockers.

I f your vacation calls for staying in an authentic log cabin, then look no further than Country Cabins. Set in the beautiful Maggie Valley, these authentic log cabins feature wood-burning fireplaces, cozy country kitchens and comfortable accommodations for 2 to 10 people.

Choices include a 150-year-old efficiency cabin with a double bed, kitchenette and gas log fireplace, great for a private retreat or a honeymoon; a one-bedroom cabin with a separate sleeping loft, fireplace and kitchen, for up to 5 people; or a 150-year-old, two-bedroom cabin that sleeps up to 10 people, with a fireplace, kitchen and laundry facilities.

Spend the day relaxing in a rocking chair on your own covered porch, or take a walk by the stream with your dog. If you want to explore the town, you are only a short distance from craft shops, restaurants and the Stompin' Grounds, a popular place to enjoy mountain music and clog dancers. For those who love the outdoors, there is great trout fishing and the Cataloochee Ski Area, all within a 5-mile radius.

Maggie Mountain Villas and Chalet

Maggie Mountain Villas and Chalet
Country Club Estates
160 Ivy Lane
Maggie Valley, NC 28751
800-308-1808 ▪ (704) 452-4285

Room Rates:	$90–$255; weekly rates available.
Pet Charges or Deposits:	$6 per stay; call for deposit. Manager's approval required.
Rated: 3 Paws 🐾🐾🐾	2 villas with 2 bedrooms accommodating up to 6 guests, each with complete kitchen, covered deck, mountain views, barbecue area, fireplace, laundry facilities and air conditioning. 1 chalet with 3 bedrooms, including a loft, 2 full baths, complete kitchen, laundry facilities, and den with fireplace.

Set in the picturesque Maggie Valley is the charming Maggie Mountain Villas and Chalet. Here guests will find secluded, peaceful wooded retreats, where you can escape for a relaxing weekend or a leisurely vacation. You may choose from two furnished villas that can accommodate up to six people. Each offers a fully equipped kitchen, separate dining area, laundry facilities, wood-burning fireplace and even the linens.

The chalet has 1,500 square feet of living space, is fully air conditioned, with three bedrooms, including a large loft, two full baths, fully equipped kitchen, laundry facilities and a large den with a cozy fireplace. Each chalet boasts a large deck with rockers or a porch swing, perfect for a lazy afternoon or a family cookout. All are completely private, and located near many major attractions and recreation areas. You and your dog will appreciate the spacious outdoors, where you can roam the hills and enjoy all that nature has to offer.

Marshall House Bed and Breakfast Inn

Marshall House Bed and Breakfast Inn
5 Hill Street
Marshall, NC 28753
(704) 649-9205

Room Rates:	$40–$75, including full breakfast.
Pet Charges or Deposits:	None. Manager's approval required.
Rated: 3 Paws 🐾🐾🐾	9 guest rooms, 2 with private baths, 1 with fireplace and private entrance, cable television and VCR in upstairs living room.

Set in the Appalachian Mountains on the banks of the beautiful French River is the quaint town of Marshall, home of the historic Marshall House Bed and Breakfast Inn. Built in 1903, the inn offers guests nine lovely guest rooms furnished in period antiques with double or single beds, two with private baths, and one room with a fireplace and a private entrance.

Constructed of pebble dash, the inn has a formal dining room with original pocket doors and a formal parlor downstairs, as well as an upstairs living room with cable television and VCR. The inn is adorned with crystal chandeliers, antiques, period furniture and collectibles.

For those looking for adventure, there is whitewater rafting, horseback riding, hiking, fishing, golf and winter snow skiing nearby.

The resident dog, Tar, will gladly show your pooch all of his favorite places on the property to play and share a biscuit or two. Owners Jim and Ruth Boylan say, "All guests that come as strangers leave as friends."

The Village at Nags Head – Village Realty

The Village at Nags Head – Village Realty
PO Box 1807
Nags Head, NC 27959
800-548-9688 ▪ (919) 480-2224

Room Rates:	$500–$5,500 weekly.
Pet Charges or Deposits:	$75 per stay, plus refundable security deposit. Limit 2 pets.
Rated: 5 Paws 🐾🐾🐾🐾🐾	24 condos and houses, luxuriously furnished, fully equipped kitchens, housekeeping services, linens and towels, televisions, VCRs, outdoor grills, fireplaces, outdoor showers, many with membership privileges at the private oceanfront Beach Club.

The tranquil waterfront of the Roanoke Sound is home to The Village at Nags Head – Village Realty. Here you will find more than 200 of the finest accommodations located within the Village community, plus the oceanfront Beach Club and the Nags Head Golf Links. Twenty-four of these allow you to bring your pet.

Choose from a wide variety of well-appointed, spacious, custom-built homes and condos that are luxuriously furnished, have fully equipped kitchens, housekeeping services, including all linens and towels, and are ready for your arrival. Many of the accommodations have private decks with beautiful ocean views, private swimming pools, large hot tubs, outdoor showers, grills, televisions, VCRs and fireplaces. Guest membership privileges are available at the private oceanfront Beach Club—featuring an Olympic-sized pool, private beach access, tennis courts and gift shops—as well as at the Nags Head Golf Links.

Holiday Inn – Dortches

Holiday Inn – Dortches
5350 Dortches Boulevard
Rocky Mount, NC 27804
(919) 937-6300

Room Rates:	$55–$70, including a limited hot breakfast. AAA, AARP, AKC and ABA discounts.
Pet Charges or Deposits:	Small and medium pets only.
Rated: 3 Paws 🐾🐾🐾	154 spacious rooms with double or king-sized beds, cable television, individual climate control, movie and sports channel, some with microwaves, refrigerators and coffee makers, laundry facilities, outdoor pool and restaurant.

Conveniently located near shopping and local attractions, the Holiday Inn – Dortches offers guests comfortable accommodations featuring double or king-sized beds, in-room movies and individual climate control. Some rooms also offer the convenience of in-room microwaves, refrigerators and coffee makers, but all have a friendly, relaxed atmosphere.

Start your day off with the complimentary hot breakfast, take advantage of the convenient room service or feast on an array of breakfast dishes served every day at Blake's Restaurant. The inn's swimming pool is the perfect place to relax with a good book or swim a few laps. In the evening, sip a cocktail in the cozy Blake's Lounge before heading to Blake's Restaurant for an array of appetizers and a full dinner menu.

The Carrier Houses Bed and Breakfast

The Carrier Houses Bed and Breakfast
249 and 255 North Main Street
Rutherfordton, NC 28139
(704) 287-4222

Room Rates: $60, including full breakfast.
Pet Charges or Deposits: $10 per stay. Manager's approval required.
Rated: 3 Paws 🐾🐾🐾 6 rooms and 2 suites, 2 with feather mattresses, private baths, fireplaces, telephones, and televisions upon request.

T he Carrier Houses Bed and Breakfast consists of two houses: the Carrier-McBrayer House with three bedrooms, currently the residence of the owners, and the Carrier-Ward House with five bedrooms, a common sitting and reception room, fully equipped kitchen and a large dining room.

Built side-by-side in 1837, the houses have been refurbished to their original state and are listed on the National Register of homes. Guests will appreciate the unique atmosphere of this unusual inn, and feel like they are right at home. It is a great place to get away, whether you are in the area to see the sights, to do some snow skiing or just passing through on business. Whatever the reason, you and your dog will enjoy not only the area, but the friendly Southern hospitality.

The Barkley House Bed and Breakfast

The Barkley House Bed and Breakfast
2522 North Carolina Highway 16 South
Taylorsville, NC 28681
(704) 632-9060

Room Rates:	$55–$79, including full breakfast; third night free when mentioning *Pets Welcome*.
Pet Charges or Deposits:	None. Manager's approval required. Small pets only; one per room.
Rated: 4 Paws 🐾🐾🐾🐾	4 guest rooms with private baths, feather mattresses, a common refrigerator for guests and a cozy den with fireplace. Pet beds available upon request.

When looking for old-fashioned Southern charm and comfort, you need look no further than the Barkley House Bed and Breakfast. Life at the inn is homey and relaxed. Guests are encouraged to kick off their shoes, prop up their feet and relax by the cozy fire in the den. Comfort is of the utmost importance. There is a "Pillow Buffet" where you may select the pillow that meets your needs. You may choose from king, full or twin beds, all with feather mattresses and plush comforters. When it comes to the bedding, the sheets are hung on the line to dry in the sunshine, to give them that wonderful scent of the fresh outdoors. Pets will appreciate the added touch of a special bed with clean sheets just for them.

Awake to a large country breakfast of piping hot coffee, tea, hot chocolate or hot apple cider served with a haystack of eggs, breakfast casserole or omelets, biscuits, gravy, grits, juice, fresh fruit, honey or jelly. There is even a breakfast banana split. You may request a pot of hot coffee or tea to be sent to your room in the morning to help you start your day.

Anderson Guest House

Anderson Guest House
520 Orange Street
Wilmington, NC 28401
888-265-1216 ▪ (910) 343-8128

Room Rates:	$85, including full breakfast.
Pet Charges or Deposits:	None. Manager's approval required.
Rated: 3 Paws 🐾🐾🐾	2 guest rooms with private baths, fireplace, ceiling fan and individual heating and air conditioning.

Wilmington is the location of the Cape Fear River, the principal deep-water port of North Carolina, and home of the Anderson Guest House. This private inn offers guests their choice of two charming rooms overlooking the garden in historic downtown Wilmington. Each room has a working fireplace, ceiling fan and individual heating and air conditioning.

Guests will enjoy a full country breakfast before heading out for the day. The historical town of Wilmington was the Colonial capital in 1743 and the scene of the 1765 Stamp Act resistance. Make sure you take a trip on a paddlewheel boat, visit the historic district or one of the many museums in the area. The Cape Fear River offers the opportunity for you and your dog to explore miles of white sandy beaches. Visit Carolina Beach, Kire Beach and Wrightsville Beach, where you can go fishing, swimming, surfing and water skiing.

North Carolina

Please Note: *Pets must be on a leash at all times and may be restricted to certain areas. For directions, use fees, pet charges and general information, contact the numbers listed below.*

National Parks

Great Smoky Mountains National Park encompasses 520,000 acres of parkland in both North Carolina and Tennessee. It is the largest protected land area east of the Rocky Mountains. Visitors will find camping facilities, picnic areas, hiking trails, fishing, nature programs and a visitors' center. For more information, call (423) 436-1200.

National Forest General Information

U.S. Forest Service
PO Box 2750
Asheville, NC 28802

800-280-2267 – reservations
(704) 257-4200 – information

National Forests

ASHEVILLE

Nantahala National Forest, located near Asheville, consists of 525,897 acres of parkland and 10 rivers. Nantahala is a Cherokee word meaning "land of the noonday sun." There are 600 miles of roads and trails, including the Appalachian Trail, running through the forest's interior. Visitors will find camping facilities, picnic areas, hiking and bicycle trails, ramps for boating, fishing and swimming. For more information, call (704) 257-4200.

Pisgah National Forest, in the western North Carolina, has 500,085 acres of parkland divided in two segments. There are two main mountain chains and several lesser ranges with several peaks over 6,000 feet high. Part of the Appalachian Trail winds along the northwestern boundary. Visitors to the park will find camping facilities, picnic areas, hiking and bicycle trails, fishing, swimming and a visitors' center. For more information, call (704) 257-4200.

NEW BERN

Croaton National Forest, located southeast of New Bern, encompasses 157,851 acres consisting mostly of pine and swamp hardwoods. There are estuaries, waterfowl nesting areas and public beaches. The area wildlife consists of black bears, alligators, woodpeckers, owls, bald eagles and falcons. Visitors will find camping facilities, picnic areas, hiking trails, ramps for boating, fishing and swimming. For more information, call (919) 638-5628.

PIEDMONT

Uwharrie National Forest, in Central North Carolina, has 47,615 acres of park-land. The forest is traversed by the Uwharrie, Yadkin and Pee Dee Rivers and borders the 8,000-acre Badin Lake near Troy. Visitors will find camping facilities, picnic areas, hiking trails, ramps for boating, fishing and swimming. For more information, call (910) 576-6391.

National Seashores

Cape Hatteras National Seashore covers approximately 45 square miles on North Carolina's Outer Banks. It is the most extensive stretch of undeveloped seashore on the Atlantic Coast. There are a few villages on the islands, but the majority is a national recreation area that includes Ocracoke and Hatteras Islands, as well as part of Bodie Island, all connected by a bridge and a ferry. Visitors will find bottlenose dolphins, vast expanses of beaches and water, as well as camping facilities, picnic areas, hiking trails, ramps for boating, fishing, swimming, nature programs and a visitors' center. For more information, call (919) 473-2111 or 441-5711.

Army Corps of Engineers

HENDERSON

John H. Kerr Reservoir, located north of Henderson on the Virginia border off I-85, consists of 106,860 acres of recreational area with camping facilities, picnic areas, hiking trails, ramps for boating, boat rentals, fishing, swimming, water skiing, nature programs and a visitors' center.

WILKESBORO

W. Kerr Scott Dam and Reservoir, located 4 miles west of Wilkesboro off SR 268 West, has 1,470 acres of recreational area with camping facilities, picnic areas, hiking trails, ramps for boating, fishing, swimming, nature programs and a visitors' center.

State Park General Information

North Carolina Division of Parks and Recreation
PO Box 27687
Raleigh, NC 27611
(919) 733-7275 or 733-4181

State Parks

ALBEMARLE

Morrow Mountain State Park, 5 miles east of Albemarle via SR 24, SR 27, SR 73 and SR 1719 near Badin in the Uwharrie Mountains on the Pee Dee River, has 4,693 acres of scenic parkland. Visitors will find camping facilities, picnic areas, hiking trails, ramps for boating, boat rentals, fishing, swimming, nature programs and a visitors' center. For more information, call (704) 982-4402.

APEX

Jordan Lake State Park, located 10 miles west of Apex off US 64, consists of 47,000 acres of parkland offering visitors camping facilities, picnic areas, hiking trails, ramps for boating, boat rentals, fishing, swimming and nature programs. For more information, call (919) 362-0586.

ASHEVILLE

Mount Mitchell State Park, located 35 miles northeast, via Blue Ridge Parkway, to SR 128 at Milepost 355, consists of 1,677 acres of scenic parkland. The summit of Mount Mitchell is 6,684 feet, the highest peak east of the Mississippi River. Visitors will find camping facilities, picnic areas, hiking trails and nature programs. For more information, call (704) 675-4611.

CRESWELL

Pettigrew State Park, located 6 miles south of Creswell off US 64, encompasses 17,743 acres of scenic parkland containing sections of an old plantation. Lake Phelps is a cypress-tree-lined wildlife sanctuary within the park. Visitors will also find camping facilities, picnic areas, hiking trails, ramps for boating, fishing and nature programs. For more information, call (919) 797-4475.

DANBURY

Hanging Rock State Park, located 4 miles northwest of Danbury off SR 89, has 6,340 acres of rugged mountain terrain with sparkling springs, waterfalls and a lake. Visitors will also find 300 species of mountain flora, camping facilities, picnic areas, hiking trails, boat rentals, fishing, swimming and nature programs. For more information, call (910) 593-8480.

DURHAM

Eno River State Park, located 3 miles northwest of Durham off CR 1569, is a 2,284-acre park with a fast-flowing river surrounded by rugged, forested hills. It has camping facilities, picnic areas, hiking trails, fishing, canoeing and nature programs. For more information, call (919) 383-1686.

ELIZABETHTOWN

Jones Lake State Park, located at 113 Jones Lake Drive, 4 miles north of Elizabethtown off SR 242, is a 2,208-acre park offering camping facilities, picnic areas, hiking trails, boat, canoe and paddleboat rentals, fishing, swimming and nature programs. For more information, call (910) 588-4550.

GATESVILLE

Merchants Millpond State Park, 6 miles northeast of Gatesville on SR 1403, encompasses 2,921 acres, where coastal ponds and swamp forest mingle to create one of North Carolina's rarest ecological communities. It also has camping facilities, picnic areas, hiking trails, boat rentals, fishing, nature programs and a visitors' center. For more information, call (919) 357-1191.

KINGS MOUNTAIN

Crowders Mountain State Park, off SR 1125 at 522 Park Office Lane, is a 2,758-acre park that includes the 1,625-foot Crowders Mountain, the 1,705-foot Kings Pinnacle and a 9-acre lake. Visitors will find camping facilities, picnic areas, hiking trails, fishing and nature programs. For more information, call (704) 853-5375.

KURE BEACH

Fort Fisher State Historic Site, 2 miles south of Kure Beach off Highway 421, consists of 287 acres of historic parkland. The fort is one of the largest Confederate earthwork fortifications and was the site of the Civil War's heaviest land-sea battle, fought January 13–15, 1865. More than two million pounds of projectiles were shot in two separate attacks. Visitors will find a monument commemorating the battle, guided tours, an audiovisual presentation, as well as hiking trails, fishing, swimming and nature programs. For more information, call (910) 458-5538.

LAKE WACCAMAW

Lake Waccamaw State Park, 6 miles south of Lake Waccamaw off US 74 and US 76, consists of 10,670 acres with one of the most unique bodies of water in the world. There are plants and animals here that are found nowhere else. Visitors will also find camping facilities, picnic areas, hiking trails, boating, fishing and nature programs. For more information, call (910) 646-4748.

LILLINGTON

Raven Rock State Park, 6 miles northwest of Lillington off US 421 on SR 1314 at Raven Rock Road, encompasses 3,058 acres of parkland with 11 miles of hiking trails, 7 miles of bridle trails, as well as camping facilities, picnic areas, fishing and nature programs. For more information, call (910) 893-4888.

MAGGIE VALLEY

Lake James State Park, 5 miles northeast of Marion on Highway 126, is a 6,500-acre park with 150 miles of shoreline surrounding the 585 acre James Lake. Visitors will find camping facilities, picnic areas, hiking trails, ramps for boating, canoe rentals, fishing, swimming and nature programs. For more information, call (704) 659-8911.

MORGANTON

South Mountain State Park, located 13 miles south of Morganton, encompasses 13,000 acres with 14 miles of trout streams, 48 miles of trails for mountain bikes, horses and hiking, as well as camping facilities, picnic areas and nature programs. For more information, call (704) 433-4772.

RALEIGH

William B. Umstead State Park, located 10 miles northwest of Raleigh off US 70, offers 5,337 acres of parkland with three small lakes, as well as camping facilities, picnic areas, hiking, bicycle and horse trails, boat rentals, fishing, swimming and nature programs. For more information, call (919) 787-3033.

WAKE FOREST

Falls Lake State Park is located at 13304 Creedmoor Road. The park is one of the state's largest recreation areas, consisting of 38,000 acres. Visitors will find camping facilities, picnic areas, hiking trails, ramps for boating, boat rentals, fishing, swimming and other water sports, nature programs and a visitors' center. For more information, call (916) 676-1027.

WASHINGTON

Goose Creek State Park, located 8 miles east of Washington on US 264, consists of 1,598 acres of varied plant life, a diversity of wetlands and habitats, as well as nine miles of shoreline on the Pamlico River. It also has find camping facilities, picnic areas, hiking, ramps for boating, fishing, swimming and nature programs. For more information, call (919) 923-2191.

South Carolina

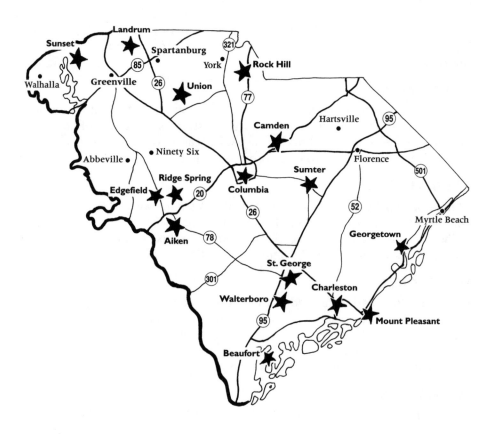

PETS WELCOME!

South Carolina

The Holley House

The Holley House
235 Richland Avenue
Aiken, SC 29801
(803) 648-4265

Room Rates:	Call for current rates. Includes continental breakfast.
Pet Charges or Deposits:	Credit card as deposit. AAA and AARP discounts.
Rated: 3 Paws 🐾🐾🐾	55 guest rooms and 15 spacious suites with double or queen beds, refrigerators, microwaves, color cable television and pool.

L ocated in historic downtown Aiken, known as the "all-American city," is the "pet friendly" Holley House. Built in 1927, the hotel has recently been totally renovated. Guest accommodations include refrigerators, microwaves and color cable television in comfortable guest rooms or spacious suites.

Start off your day with your complimentary continental breakfast before visiting some of the local historic sights and attractive gardens, swimming in the hotel pool or strolling through the courtyard with your dog.

Battery Creek Inn

Battery Creek Inn
19 Marina Village Lane
Beaufort, SC 29902
(803) 521-1441

Room Rates:	$78; weekly rates available. AAA discounts.
Pet Charges or Deposits:	$50 per stay; $50 deposit.
Rated: 3 Paws 🐾🐾🐾	20 suites, private entrances, fully equipped kitchens, outstanding views, cable television and private parking.

Located across from the gates of Parris Island is the waterfront Battery Creek Inn, where you will find delightfully furnished guest suites. Located directly on the waterfront, near the Battery marina, the guest rooms offer private entrances, fully equipped kitchens and outstanding views of Battery Creek and the Intracoastal Waterway.

The Battery Creek Inn is convenient to golf courses, the downtown historic district, Hunting Island State Park and the beaches. Here you and your dog have over 5,000 acres on which to picnic, hike, fish or swim.

Carolina Oaks Bed and Breakfast

Carolina Oaks Bed and Breakfast
127 Union Street
Camden, SC 29020
(803) 432-2366

Room Rates:	$85–$125, including a full breakfast.
Pet Charges or Deposits:	$25 per stay; $50 deposit. Manager's approval required.
Rated: 4 Paws 🐾🐾🐾🐾	3 guest rooms, 1 cottage/suite, all with fireplaces, featherbeds, antique quilts, down comforters, central air conditioning. Terry robes provided.

Set in the heart of Camden's historic district is the charming, Federal-style Carolina Oaks Bed and Breakfast Inn, built in the early 1900s. This spacious home in a quiet setting provides a convenient and interesting stepping-off point to other fine homes, wonderful restaurants and Camden's festivals.

In the main house, guests will find well designed, comfortable guest rooms decorated with period antiques and soft textures, antique quilts, down comforters and wood-burning fireplaces.

The private cottage is furnished in antiques with a queen-sized brass bed, freshly ironed cotton bed linens, antique quilts and soft down comforters. The cottage has a separate living room and full kitchen.

Breakfasts are served on damask linen with homemade treats such as fresh jams and preserves, with breads still hot from the oven, omelets laced with Canadian bacon, three kinds of cheese and fresh-picked herbs, an assortment of seasonal fresh fruit and piping hot coffee or tea.

Town and Country Inn and Conference Center

Town and Country Inn and Conference Center
2008 Savannah Highway
Charleston, SC 29407
800-334-6660 ▪ (803) 571-1000

Room Rates:	$59–$179; AAA and AARP discounts.
Pet Charges or Deposits:	None.
Rated: 3 Paws 🐾🐾🐾	III guest rooms and deluxe suites, outdoor pool and gazebo, saunas, whirlpool, racquetball courts, health club, some kitchens with microwaves and refrigerators, laundry facilities, room service, restaurant and cocktail lounge, airport transportation and golf privileges at 15 area courses.

L ocated in historic Charleston near the Ashley River is the Town and Country Inn and Conference Center. The guest rooms and suites are spacious, well-designed rooms.

A full-service Health Spa is available here, offering state-of-the-art weight machines, life cycles, stair steppers, men's and ladies saunas, indoor lap pool and two regulation racquetball courts.

The highly acclaimed Trotters Restaurant and Lounge offers entrées such as fluffy omelets, plantation cakes, generous sandwiches and salads as well as fresh seafood, beef and poultry specials.

While in Charleston visit the historical sites, homes and landmarks, or take your dog for a day of fun at Francis Marion National Forest, where you can hike or enjoy boating or fishing.

Adam's Mark Hotel

Adam's Mark Hotel
1200 Hampton Street
Columbia, SC 29201
800-444-ADAM ▪ (803) 771-7000

Room Rates: $79–$144; AAA, AARP, AKC and ABA discounts.
Pet Charges or Deposits: $25 refundable deposit.
Rated: 4 Paws 🐾🐾🐾🐾 300 guest rooms and 4 luxury suites all with in-room movies, cable television and clock radios. Club Level offers complimentary continental breakfast, evening hors d'oeuvres and concierge services. Free airport shuttle, indoor pool, sun deck, fitness center, whirlpool, gift shop, valet service, guest laundry, room service, restaurant, sports bar and cocktail lounge.

L ocated downtown near the State Capitol and the University of South Carolina, the Adam's Mark Hotel offers well-designed rooms with all the amenities expected in a premier hotel—amenities such as concierge services, access to a private Club Lounge, complimentary continental breakfast, evening hors d'oeuvres and your morning news papers.

The Adam's Mark Hotel offers a fitness center with whirlpool, sun deck and pool. The hotel is close to several parks.

Cedar Grove Plantation Bed and Breakfast

Cedar Grove Plantation Bed and Breakfast
1365 Highway 25, North
Edgefield, SC 29824
(803) 637-3056

Room Rates:	$55–$75, including full breakfast.
Pet Charges or Deposits:	One night's room rate as deposit. Manager's approval required.
Rated: 3 Paws 🐾🐾🐾	2 guest rooms with private baths, fireplaces, television and VCR, swimming pool, hot tub/spa, herb and flower garden.

L ocated just outside of town, the Cedar Grove Plantation Bed and Breakfast was built in 1790 by John Blocker. Listed on the National Register of Historic Places, it is one of the oldest plantation houses in the Upstate. The house still retains most of the original features, such as the hand-carved mantels and moldings, fireplaces in every room, lovely hand-painted French wallpaper in the parlor, and a unique barrel-vaulted entry ceiling in the hallway. The original kitchen and slave quarters still stand today.

The Blocker Suite features a separate sitting room with television and VCR. The downstairs guest room will accommodate two people, but be forewarned: it is already occupied by a ghost! Once you have made it through the night, you can tell everyone about your ghostly experiences at breakfast in the elegant dining room, or, when the weather permits, dine outdoors on the spacious back porch. Be sure to take a stroll through the plantation's herb and flower garden with your dog, a favorite stopping spot for the local deer, fox and wild turkeys.

Mansfield Plantation
Bed and Breakfast Country Inn

Mansfield Plantation Bed and Breakfast Country Inn
1776 Mansfield Road
Georgetown, SC 29440
800-355-3223 ▪ (803) 546-6961

Room Rates:	$95–$115, including a full breakfast.
Pet Charges or Deposits:	None.
Rated: 5 Paws 🐾🐾🐾🐾🐾	5 main-house guest rooms furnished in antiques with full private baths, fireplaces and private entrances; 3 guest houses with full private baths and working fireplaces.

Moonlight and Magnolias. The Mansfield Plantation is a historic pre-Civil War plantation situated on 900 private acres. The avenue of noble live oak trees draped in Spanish moss leads you to the traditional ante-bellum plantation house which is furnished with antiques. This historic rice plantation, located in the heart of South Carolina's Tidelands, was once the exclusive haunt of aristocrats, and is now open to discriminating guests.

Three charming guest houses feature private entrances, handsome furnishings, floral chintz fabrics, fireplaces with beautifully carved mantelpieces and woodwork and full private baths.

Situated on the Black River, the 900 private acres are a naturalist's paradise, offering guests and their pets a private getaway. Walk in the woods, explore the old rice fields, fish from the private dock, go boating on the river, or picnic on the sandy shores. The serene environment and elegant atmosphere blend beautifully to make your visit a lasting memory.

The Red Horse Inn

The Red Horse Inn
310 North Campbell Road
Landrum, SC 29356
(864) 895-4968

Room Rates:	$85, additional guest $10 each, continental breakfast included. Weekly rate available.
Pet Charges or Deposits:	$25 deposit. Small dogs only. Horses welcome. Manager's approval required.
Rated: 5 Paws 🐾🐾🐾🐾🐾	5 cottages with kitchens, separate bedrooms, private baths, sleeping lofts, separate living rooms with fireplace, decks or patios, some with Jacuzzis, color television, air conditioning.

Set on 190 acres with trails, streams, fields and ponds in the midst of equestrian country is the delightful Red Horse Inn. Sweeping mountain views, pastoral vistas and endless sky offer the perfect backdrop to each season.

The charming, romantic Victorian cottages are exquisitely furnished and decorated offering a kitchen, bedroom, bath, sleeping loft, living room with fireplace, decks or patios, color television and air-conditioning. A breakfast basket is provided each morning for your room.

Local attractions include two championship golf courses, horseback riding, hiking, fishing, antiquing, bird hunting, sporting clay course and the Foothills Equestrian Nature Center. The spring, summer and fall come alive with various events and festivals.

Comfort Inn East

Comfort Inn East
310 Highway 17 Bypass
Mount Pleasant, SC 29464
800-228-5150 ▪ (803) 884-5853

Room Rates:	$69 and up, including continental breakfast. AAA and AARP discounts.
Pet Charges or Deposits:	$10 per stay. Manager's approval required.
Rated: 3 Paws ❀❀❀	120 guest rooms and 2 luxury suites, some with whirlpools, all with cable television, swimming pool and laundry facilities.

I f you are looking for convenient, comfortable, affordable accommodations with professional and courteous service, the Comfort Inn East may be for you. Centrally located in the midst of Fort Sumter National Monument, near Charleston, with all of its historical attractions, leisure activities and the Atlantic Coast beaches and harbor, you will find plenty of activities to keep you entertained.

The inn features an exercise facility and pool. Pets are welcome guests and will enjoy the spacious grounds. Sassy, the resident dog, will be happy to show them around.

Southwood Manor Bed and Breakfast

Southwood Manor Bed and Breakfast
100 East Main Street
Ridge Spring, SC 29129
(803) 685-5100

Room Rates:	$65–$85, including a full breakfast. AAA and AARP discounts.
Pet Charges or Deposits:	None. Horses welcome. Manager's approval required.
Rated: 5 Paws 🐾🐾🐾🐾🐾	4 spacious rooms and 1 suite with fine antiques, four-poster beds, air conditioning, color television, fireplaces, full baths, swimming pool and private air strip.

Surrounded by the flavors of the true South, with cotton fields, pecan groves and a working cotton gin, is the Southwood Manor Bed and Breakfast. This magnificent Georgian Colonial plantation is located in the sleepy country town of Ridge Spring, offering a relaxed atmosphere and gracious accommodations.

The large guest rooms are furnished with queen-sized four-poster beds and period antiques. Start your day with a full country breakfast in the formal dining room, or dine in the privacy of your room.

If relaxation is what you have planned, you have come to the right place. Just imagine sipping fresh lemonade as you lounge poolside. For those who crave an active vacation, set up a game of tennis on the inn's court, try your hand at billiards, or practice your putting, all on site, followed by a sherry on the curved and columned portico. Your dog will appreciate the quarter-acre fenced-in yard, and your horse has two box stalls and a pasture.

Park Avenue Inn Bed and Breakfast

Park Avenue Inn Bed and Breakfast
347 Park Avenue
Rock Hill, SC 29730
(803) 325-1764

Room Rates: $60–$75, including a continental breakfast.
Pet Charges or Deposits: Call for deposits. Small pets only. Manager's approval required.
Rated: 3 Paws 🐾🐾🐾 3 guest rooms, each with private bath, uniquely furnished with antiques and canopy beds.

Built in 1916, the Park Avenue Inn Bed and Breakfast offers guests three uniquely furnished guest rooms. Each room has a private bath, some with six-foot-long bathtubs. Antiques and hand-crafted canopy beds add to the decor.

The inn features twin parlors and an oversized front porch with a swing and a rocker, an ideal location for freshly made lemonade or iced tea. A continental breakfast is served, either in the large dining area with a ten-foot-long pine table, or, in your room. The resident Pomeranians, Tiki and Toby, will gladly show your dog all of their favorite places to play.

Holiday Inn

Holiday Inn
6014 West Jim Bilton Boulevard
St. George, SC 29477
800-HOLIDAY ▪ (803) 563-4581

Room Rates:	$69–$75, including a full breakfast. AAA, AARP, AKC and ABA discounts.
Pet Charges or Deposits:	None.
Rated: 3 Paws 🐾🐾🐾	120 guest rooms with cable television, in-room movies, outdoor swimming pool, kiddie pool, laundry facilities, complimentary breakfast and luncheon buffet, restaurant and cocktail lounge.

N estled in the serene Low Country, only an hour from historic Charleston and Columbia, the state capital, is the Holiday Inn. Combining a warm atmosphere and an attentive staff, you will find true Southern hospitality in an establishment that offers amenities normally found in a large hotel. The hospitality of the staff extends to their four-legged guests as well. This pet-friendly inn even has a large area for your canine friends to romp and play.

A full breakfast is included in your room rate. Nightly specials at the Whistle Stop Restaurant feature Southern cuisine and a wide variety of spirits.

Magnolia House Bed and Breakfast

Magnolia House Bed and Breakfast
230 Church Street
Sumter, SC 29150
800-666-0296 ▪ (803) 775-6694

Room Rates:	$65–$125, including full breakfast. AAA discount.
Pet Charges or Deposits:	$65 deposit. Manager's approval required.
Rated: 5 Paws 🐾🐾🐾🐾🐾	5 charming rooms and 1 suite, most with fireplaces, stained glass windows, inlaid oak floors, each room decorated in a different era; refreshments in formal garden. Resident pets.

Make yourself at home in the Greek Revival-style Magnolia House Bed and Breakfast Inn with its 5 fireplaces, stained glass windows and inlaid oak floors. Located in the historic district of Sumter, you enter the home expecting to see ladies in flowing gowns and men wearing evening coats. The details of the decorating are tasteful as well as entertaining. There are delightful vignettes at every turn.

Each of the inviting guest rooms is decorated in antiques from a different era with comfortable upholstered chairs and hand-made quilts and the thickest towels you will find. A full breakfast is served in the large dining room, decorated with beautiful French antiques.

This historic home, with its Corinthian columns, wraparound porches with overstuffed chairs and cypress swings, invites you to relax with complimentary afternoon refreshments. The garden blooms year-round with roses, tulips, magnolias and scented gardenias. A collection of birdhouses and feeders encourages a large variety of birds to stop for a visit.

Laurel Springs Country Inn

Laurel Springs Country Inn
1137 Moorefield Memorial Highway
Sunset, SC 29685
(864) 878-2252

Room Rates:	$100–$200
Pet Charges or Deposits:	1 night's room rate as deposit. Manager's approval required.
Rated: 3 Paws ❧❧❧	2 waterfront, non-smoking log cabins with kitchens.

T he Laurel Springs Country Inn is a place to come and relax. Here you can get away from the hustle and bustle of the world and escape to a time gone by. Submerge yourself in nature with your own private log cabin in a forest setting. These uniquely decorated cabins offer you all the luxuries of home.

Spend your day relaxing and fishing with your dog at the inn's private pond. Sorry dogs, no swimming is allowed—this pond is reserved for the resident ducks. Minutes from the inn are mountain streams and trout farms, as well as nature trails to explore, including the ones at Table Rock National Park. Many local farms offer horseback riding.

A short drive from the inn is the Chattooga and Nantahala Rivers for whitewater rafting through cool forests and rock flumes. Finish your day with a soothing massage, a late night bonfire, or curl up with a good book and a glass of wine in front of your own fireplace.

Juxa Plantation

Juxa Plantation
117 Wilson Road
Union, SC 29379
(864) 427-8688

Room Rates:	$85, including a full breakfast.
Pet Charges or Deposits:	$100 deposit. Call for nightly fees. Manager's approval required.
Rated: 4 Paws 🐾🐾🐾🐾	3 guest rooms and 1 large suite furnished in antiques, with private baths.

Built in the early 1800s by the MacGregors, a Scottish clan fleeing a failed conspiracy against the King, the Juxa Plantation has been lovingly restored to its original beauty. Nestled among ancient oaks and magnolia trees, this 150-year-old mansion is furnished with beautiful antiques, many of which are available for purchase. The lovely guest rooms offer lots of Southern charm with private baths. The blend of country and luxury makes Juxa Plantation the perfect choice for a romantic getaway or a relaxing weekend.

Step back into a time when life moved at a slower pace. Guests are welcome to stroll the exquisite grounds, explore the wooded path and share a bit of the family's history as you read the old headstones in the family cemetery.

Mt. Carmel Farm Bed and Breakfast

Mt. Carmel Farm Bed and Breakfast
Route 2, Box 580-A
Walterboro, SC 29488
(803) 538-5770

Room Rates:	$75, including full breakfast and light dinner.
Pet Charges or Deposits:	None for cats and dogs. $15 per horse, per day; $20 for each additional horse.
Rated: 4 Paws 🐾🐾🐾🐾	2 guest rooms with two doubles or a queen-sized bed, private baths, ceiling fans, pet blankets and bowls in each room, formal dining room, front and back porches, pool, barn and paddock area. Dogs, horses and pot-bellied pigs in residence.

I f you are looking for a homey country setting for your next getaway, consider the Mt. Carmel Farm Bed and Breakfast. This inn is more like visiting Grandma's house. From the minute you arrive at the front gate, the aroma of fresh-baked goods drifts through the air. The well-decorated guest rooms have private baths and a queen or two double beds with cozy afghans. The larger room overlooks the back field and paddock area. Both rooms have fluffy blankets and bowls for your pet.

Start your day off with a big country breakfast of fresh cinnamon buns, cheese danish or blueberry cake served in the large country kitchen, where everyone gathers talk to Maureen, the owner/innkeeper, as she prepares the meals.

A comfortable den with a fireplace and two porches entices you to curl up with a good book. Be sure to get a cookie from the jar for yourself, and for Eddie, the resident dog, a pat on the head. Then grab some carrots and head down to the barn to visit the horses and the pot-bellied pigs, Gus and Hammy.

WHERE TO TAKE YOUR PET IN
South Carolina

Please note: Pets must be on a leash at all times and may be restricted to certain areas. For directions, use fees, pet charges and general information, contact the numbers listed below.

National Forest General Information

US Forest Service
4931 Broad River Road
Columbia, SC 29210-4021

800-280-2267 – reservations
(803) 561-4000 – information

National Forest

CHARLESTON

Francis Marion National Forest, north of Charleston, consists of 251,000 acres of flatlands, coastal areas, black swamps and small lakes known as "Carolina Bays," thought to be meteorite impact depressions. Visitors will also find camping facilities, picnic areas, hiking and bicycle trails, boat ramps and fishing areas. For more information, call (803) 825-3387.

SUMTER

Sumter National Forest, in western South Carolina, consists of 360,000 acres of foothills in the southern Appalachians, rolling terrain in the Piedmont and the upper reaches of the Savannah River. It also has camping facilities, picnic areas, hiking and bicycle trails, ramps for boating, fishing and swimming. For more information, call (803) 561-4000.

Army Corps of Engineers

CALHOUN FALLS

Richard B. Russell Lake, 1 mile west of Calhoun Falls on SR 72, is a 26,650-acre recreation area on the Savannah River overlooking the dam and lake. Visitors will find camping facilities, picnic areas, hiking trails, ramps for boating, fishing, swimming and a visitors' center. For more information, call the Old 96 Tourism Commission at (864) 984-2233.

GREENWOOD

J. Strom Thurmond Lake, 30 miles northwest of Greenwood on US 221, is a 70,000-acre recreation area and 1,200 miles of shoreline offers visitors an aquarium with hands-on exhibits, camping facilities, picnic areas, hiking trails, ramps for boating, fishing, swimming, nature programs and a visitors' center. For more information, call (864) 333-2476.

State Park General Information

Department of Parks, Recreation and Tourism
1205 Pendleton Street
Columbia, SC 29201
(803) 734-0122

State Parks

AIKEN

Aiken State Park, 16 miles east of Aiken off US 78, has 1,067 acres on the Edisto River, where four lakes are fed by natural springs. The park offers camping facilities, picnic areas, hiking trails, ramps for boating, boat rentals, fishing and swimming. For more information, call (803) 649-2857.

BISHOPVILLE

Lee State Park, 7 miles east of Bishopville off I-20, has 2,839 acres of parkland with fishing, equestrian events, camping facilities, picnic areas, hiking trails, boating, fishing and swimming. For more information, call (803) 428-3833.

CHERAW

Cheraw State Park, 4 miles southwest of Cheraw on US 1, with 7,361 acres of sandhills in the oldest state park in South Carolina. Visitors will find an 18-hole golf course, camping facilities, picnic areas, hiking trails, ramps for boating, fishing and lake swimming. For more information, call 800-868-9630.

COLUMBIA

Lake Wateree State Park, located 30 miles north of Columbia off I-77, is a 238-acre pine-shaded island in the 14,000-acre Lake Wateree. There are 190 miles of shoreline, camping facilities, picnic areas, hiking trails, ramps for boating and fishing. For more information, call (803) 482-6126.

DILLON

Little Pee Dee State Park, 11 miles southeast of Dillon off SR 57, is an 835-acre park where the gently flowing Little Pee Dee River offers some of the state's best fishing, as well as camping facilities, picnic areas, hiking trails, boating, boat rentals and swimming. For more information, call (803) 774-8872.

EDISTO ISLAND

Edisto Beach State Park, located on Edisto Island, 50 miles southwest of Charleston on SR 174, is a 1,255-acre beachcomber's dream. The beautiful 3-mile-long beach is dotted with sand dollars and seashells. Visitors will also find marshlands, camping facilities, picnic areas, hiking trails, fishing and swimming. For more information, call (803) 869-2756.

FLORENCE

Lynches River State Park, located 13 miles southwest of Florence on US 52, consists of 668 acres of relaxing woodlands with river fishing, bird watching, picnic areas, hiking and bicycle trails, boating, boat rentals and an Olympic-sized swimming pool. For more information, call (803) 389-2785.

GREENVILLE

Caesars Head State Park, located 16 miles north of Greenville on US 276 at the South and North Carolina state line, is a 7,467-acre park featuring the beauty of the Upcountry at an elevation of 3,208 feet. There are rocky promontories, picnic areas, hiking trails, nature programs and a visitors' center. For more information, call (864) 836-6115.

Paris Mountain State Park, 6 miles north of Greenville off US 25, is a 1,275-acre area that has been protected since 1890. There are three stocked ponds for fishing, lake swimming, pedal boats, camping facilities, picnic areas and hiking trails. For more information, call (864) 244-5565.

McCORMICK

Baker Creek State Park, 4 miles southwest of McCormick on US 378, is a 1,305-acre, family-oriented park with sandy beaches, pedal boats, a carpet golf course, camping facilities, picnic areas, hiking trails, fishing and swimming. For more information, call (864) 443-2457.

MONCKS CORNER

Old Santee Canal State Park, located 1 mile east of Moncks Corner off US 52 bypass, is a 250-acre park at the southern end of the Santee Canal, which was the first canal in the Americas. Visitors will find picnic areas, hiking trails, boardwalks, ramps for boating, canoe rentals, fishing, nature programs and a visitors' center. For more information, call (803) 899-5200.

MYRTLE BEACH

Myrtle Beach State Park, located 3 miles south of Myrtle Beach on US 17, is only 312 acres, but it is one of the most popular parks in the state. It offers camping facilities, picnic areas, hiking trails, fishing, ocean and pool swimming, year-round nature and recreation programs, as well as a visitors' center. For more information, call (803) 238-5325.

OLANTA

Woods Bay State Park, 2.5 miles south of Olanta on US 301, consists of 1,541 acres with a geological mystery called Carolina Bay located in the heart of the park. The old depression in the earth holds enough water to accommodate a variety of wildlife, including alligators. There is a boardwalk for observations, as well as picnic areas, hiking trails, boating, canoe and boat rentals, fishing and nature programs. For more information, call (803) 659-4445.

PICKENS

Devils Fork State Park, located 16 miles northwest of Pickens off SR 11, consists of 644 acres on Lake Jocassee, the state's deepest and most pristine mountain waters. Visitors will also find camping facilities, picnic areas, hiking trails, ramps for boating, fishing, swimming and a visitors' center. For more information, call (864) 944-2639.

SANTEE

Santee State Park, 3 miles northwest of Santee on SC 6, consists of 2,478 acres of parkland. It has camping facilities, picnic areas, tennis courts, hiking trails, ramps for boating, boat rentals, fishing, swimming, nature-based boat tours and a visitors' center. Call (803) 854-2408 or 854-4005 for more information.

WALHALLA

Oconee Station State Park, located 12 miles northwest of Walhalla off SR 28, encompasses 1,165 acres featuring the Oconee Station, a fieldstone blockhouse built in 1792 along the South Carolina frontier. The park also has camping facilities, picnic areas, hiking trails, boating, boat rentals, fishing, swimming and a visitors' center. For more information, call (864) 638-0079.

YORK

Kings Mountain State Park, 12 miles northwest of York between SC 161 and I-85, consists of 6,471 acres of parkland on a craggy promontory where the tide of the American Revolution was turned. There is a restored 1840s frontier homestead, camping facilities, picnic areas, hiking trails, boating, boat rentals, fishing and swimming. For more information, call (803) 222-3209.

Tennessee

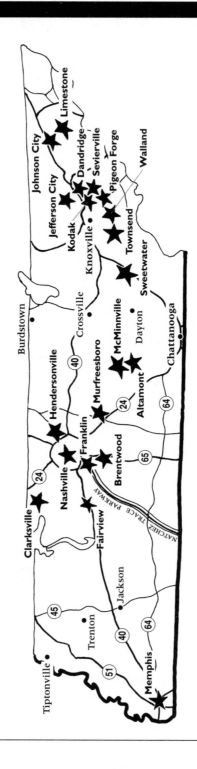

PETS WELCOME!

Tennessee

The Manor Bed and Breakfast

The Manor Bed and Breakfast
PO Box 156
Altamont, TN 37301
(615) 692-3153

Room Rates:	$55, including full breakfast and complimentary drinks.
Pet Charges or Deposits:	Call for deposit information. Manager's approval required.
Rated: 3 Paws ❖❖❖	6 guest rooms, 4 baths, picnic area, cable TV, VCR and stereo, library, 3 sitting rooms, 3 porches and a picnic area. Non-smoking inn.

Built in 1885, this 6,000-square-foot Federal-style manor served briefly as the first courthouse of Grundy County, but is best known as the former house of Fannie Moffitt, H.B. Northcutt's eccentric granddaughter, who left her entire fortune "to the wind."

The home was purchased and renovated in 1955 and opened as a restaurant and boarding house. Now listed on the National Register of Historic Places, the building has been lovingly restored to its original glory, including the acre of groomed grounds. Constructed with 19-inch-thick brick walls and set on a huge slab of limestone, The Manor is much like a fortress. The thick walls keep the rooms cool in the summer and warm in the winter, ensuring guests' comfort.

The six guest rooms, four baths and formal library are adorned with many unique and fine antiques; even breakfast is served on fine antique china with sterling silver pieces. The Manor gift shop offers a large selection of Southern antiques, collectibles and fine old glassware. Guests may adjourn to the library, filled with more than 3,000 books and a 120-year-old grand piano. The Manor's porches are also inviting places to spend a bit of leisure time.

Brentwood Hilton Suites

Brentwood Hilton Suites
9000 Overlook Boulevard
Brentwood, TN 37027
800-HILTONS ▪ (615) 370-0111

Room Rates:	$125–$155, including full breakfast and complimentary evening beverages. AAA and AARP discounts.
Pet Charges or Deposits:	None. Pets under 20 lbs.
Rated: 4 Paws 🐾🐾🐾🐾	203 spacious suites with wet bars, coffee makers, microwaves, refrigerators, free in-room movies, cable television, laundry services, heated pool, whirlpool, exercise room and restaurant.

When looking for beautifully appointed rooms with plenty of space, convenient location, that extra personal touch and most of the amenities of home, you'll find all that and more at Brentwood Hilton Suites. You will feel right at home with your in-room coffee brewer, wet bar, microwave oven, refrigerator, large dining/work area, in-room movies, cable television, plus guest laundry services. Start your day with a workout in the fitness center or a refreshing swim in the indoor pool, or take a brisk morning stroll around the grounds with your dog before feasting on your complimentary, prepared-to-order breakfast in the hotel's restaurant.

Busy guests will appreciate the convenience of the Atrium Market, where you may purchase snacks, soft drinks, spirits, souvenirs, videocassette tapes and microwaveable foods. Guests are invited to enjoy a complimentary drink at the two-hour beverage reception each evening.

Hachland Hill Inn

Hachland Hill Inn
1601 Madison Street
Clarksville, TN 37043
(615) 647-4084

Room Rates:	$65–$100
Pet Charges or Deposits:	$10 per day. Manager's approval required.
Rated: 3 Paws ❀ ❀ ❀	8 guest rooms and 3 suites, fireplaces, private entrances, showers and bath tubs. Famous dining.

T he Colonial-style Hachland Hill Inn offers guests more than just charming guest rooms and spacious suites furnished with antiques. There's also plenty of gracious Southern hospitality.

This enchanting inn offers guests unexpected pleasures. While a secluded inn 45 minutes outside of Nashville may seem an unlikely place to find Oysters Rockefeller or Chateaubriand, delectable surprises are a common occurrence at Hachland Hill.

People from around the world have been wooed by the culinary wonders prepared here. The regional flavor of dishes such as fried chicken, country ham and homemade biscuits have been handed down through generations. More cosmopolitan palates will delight in Coquilles Saint Jacques, Moroccan Leg of Lamb and other worldly dishes. The inn's grand ballroom seats up to 300 guests and adjoins a historic 1790 log home.

Guests will no doubt be tempted to take pooches for a stroll around the lovely grounds adorned with fields of wildflowers and even a bird sanctuary. Renowned author, gourmet chef and inn owner Phila Hach prides herself on making the Hachland Hill Inn one of the South's favorite destinations for charming accommodations and fine dining.

Mountain Harbor Inn

Mountain Harbor Inn
1199 Highway 139
Dandridge, TN 37725
(423) 397-3345

Room Rates:	$75–$135, including full breakfast.
Pet Charges or Deposits:	$8 per day. Manager's approval required. Call for deposit information.
Rated: 5 Paws 🐾🐾🐾🐾🐾	4 spacious rooms and 9 luxury waterfront suites located near Great Smoky Mountain National Park.

T he Mountain Harbor Inn strives for a balance between luxury, comfort and beauty. Ensconced in a scenic mountain setting on Douglas Lake, the inn's charming guest rooms are decorated with antiques and quilts. Pillared porches beckon guests to relax and enjoy the serenity and splendor of the surrounding mountains and lake.

The inn is ideal for a weekend getaway or an extended vacation. There are no time schedules here. Breakfast is served over a two-hour period to allow guests to start their day when they are ready.

No matter what season you choose to visit, each has its own beauty and special events to offer. Spend the day exploring the area with your dog, or head to town and buy one of the locally crafted rockers for your own. Boat launching and docking areas are available for those who wish to spend the day on the lake fishing for bass. There are even charter services available to take anglers to the best fishing spots.

Sweet Annie's Bed, Breakfast and Barn

Sweet Annie's Bed, Breakfast and Barn
7201 Crow Cut Road, SW
Fairview, TN 37062
888-297-3042 ▪ (615) 799-8833

Room Rates:	$55–$70, including full breakfast and nightly snack.
Pet Charges or Deposits:	$25 deposit. Must have carrier or crate for pet. Manager's approval required. Horses welcome.
Rated: 3 Paws 🐾🐾🐾	2 guest rooms that share a bathroom, bathrobes provided, in-room telephones, barbecue, library of books and videos, TV, VCR, laundry facilities, swimming pool, hot tub and tennis court. Non-smoking inn.

T he guest rooms of Sweet Annie's Bed, Breakfast and Barn are light, airy and comfortable. This contemporary inn basks in restful, pastel hues with lots of windows to bring the great outdoors inside.

After feasting on the signature breakfast of a French toast sandwich (cinnamon raisin bread filled with cream cheese and bananas), you may be tempted to sip that second cup of coffee while relaxing on the deck in a comfortable rocking chair or reclining under the shade of a maple tree in the back yard. Don't worry if you overindulge; personal fitness workouts are available here, too.

If that's not your style, try working off breakfast with a few laps in the swimming pool, or go for a walk through Bowie Nature Park's hiking and riding trails, which wind through 800 acres. You can ride one of the inn's four horses if you didn't bring your own.

Namaste Acres Barn Bed and Breakfast Inn

Namaste Acres Barn Bed and Breakfast Inn
5436 Leipers Creek Road
Franklin, TN 37064
(615) 791-0333

Room Rates:	$75–$80, including full breakfast.
Pet Charges or Deposits:	None. Must have carrier or crate for pet. Horse boarding $5–$10 per day. Trailer shuttle service available.
Rated: 4 Paws 🐾🐾🐾🐾	4 theme suites with private entrances and baths, feather-quilted queen-sized beds, large comfortable sitting area, TV, VCR, ceiling fans, large decks, hot tub, pool and refrigerators.

Nestled in the scenic valley of Leipers Fork is the Namaste Acres Barn Bed and Breakfast Inn. This Dutch Colonial country ranch welcomes both two- and four-legged guests. Choose from four theme suites, including the Franklin Quarters, with soothing tones of cream and peach compliment-ing Confederate Civil War memorabilia and art that accents that period of Southern history. The Frontier Cabin is a log cabin suite with rough-sawn lumber walls, 12-foot ceilings with hand-crafted beams and an exterior deck. The Indian Lodge is an extra-large suite decorated in a Native American motif complete with Indian artifacts and warm Southwest color schemes. If you are looking for the Old West, the Cowboy Bunkhouse is for you. Its rough-sawn lumber walls and massive log and rope bunk beds will whisk you back in time.

Hiking enthusiasts, naturalists, historians and equestrians will all enjoy the 26 miles of bridle and hiking trails at Natchez Trace, directly across from Namaste Acres.

Morning Star Bed and Breakfast

Morning Star Bed and Breakfast
460 Jones Lane
Hendersonville, TN 37075
(615) 264-2614

Room Rates:	$95–$120, including full breakfast. AAA, AARP, AKC and ABA discounts.
Pet Charges or Deposits:	None. Manager's approval required.
Rated: 4 Paws 🐾🐾🐾🐾	3 guest rooms and 1 suite, large wrap-around porches, two Par 3 practice golf tees, large patio and gazebo, high tea and complimentary beverages. Dog runs and exercise areas.

T he Morning Star Bed and Breakfast inn offers guests beautifully decorated rooms with private vanities, claw-foot tubs and showers, with brass fixtures throughout. This custom country Victorian home was featured in the January 1995 special edition of *Elite Unique Homes* magazine. Common rooms are comfortable and inviting, with four fireplaces.

A large wrap-around front porch with white wicker swings and rockers encourages guests to sit awhile and view the Nashville skyline, the sparkling city lights and colorful sunsets.

Start your day off with the complimentary full breakfast, served in the formal dining room or on the porch, before heading out for a day of adventure. Located minutes away are downtown Nashville; Opryland, home of the Grand Ole' Opry; Opryland USA Themepark; and TBN's Trinity Music City. If relaxation is what you are craving, then stay put and work on your golf game on the inn's practice range or curl up with a good book and relax with your dog in the gazebo.

Apple Valley Resort

Apple Valley Resort
1850 Paul Drive
Jefferson City, TN 37760
800-545-8106 ▪ (423) 475-3745

Room Rates:	$75–$200; weekly rates available. AAA, AARP, AKC and ABA discounts.
Pet Charges or Deposits:	Call for deposits.
Rated: 3 Paws 🐾🐾🐾	8 chalets with views of the lake or the woods, 1 or 2 bedrooms, full baths, kitchens, wood-burning stove or fireplace, televisions, VCR, boat dock or deck. All linens provided.

Just off the beaten path to the Great Smoky Mountains, the Apple Valley Resort offers lakefront and mountaintop chalets. Here you will find one- and two-bedroom chalets with full baths and kitchens, hot tubs, wood-burning fireplaces or stoves, sunny decks or your own boat dock.

Everything is provided; all you need to bring is your spirit of adventure. Spend the day exploring the mountains with your dog, fishing from the dock, Jet Skiing and swimming. Or rent a boat and venture onto Lake Cherokee, with 450 miles of shoreline, to cast a line for really big bass, catfish and stripers.

Apple Valley Resort is centrally located a few minutes from the beautiful Smoky Mountains, quaint restaurants, Dollywood, outlet shopping, antique malls and many other attractions.

Garden Plaza Hotel

Garden Plaza Hotel
211 Mockingbird Lane
Johnson City, TN 37604
800-3-GARDEN ▪ (423) 929-2000

Room Rates:	$79–$120. AAA, AARP, AKC and ABA discounts.
Pet Charges or Deposits:	None. Manager's approval required.
Rated: 4 Paws 🐾🐾🐾🐾	183 spacious rooms and 3 luxury suites, cable television, heated indoor/outdoor pool, whirlpool, health club privileges, valet laundry, airport transportation, restaurant and cocktail lounge.

I f you are looking for a full-service hotel with Southern hospitality, then experience what the Garden Plaza Hotel has to offer. From the distinctive, comfortable rooms and affordable rates to the in-house dining, the home-grown attention to detail is unsurpassed. Centrally located near many historic areas, business communities, attractions, scenic parks, unique shops and challenging golf courses, the Garden Plaza Hotel is a perfect choice for those traveling on a short business trip or an extended vacation.

Spend your day relaxing by the pool with a good book, exploring the wonders of area attractions or romping with your dog at one of the local parks.

For your dining pleasure, Ezra's, the hotel's in-house restaurant, offers a wide variety of dining delights.

Dumplin Valley Inn – Best Western

Dumplin Valley Inn – Best Western
3426 Winfield Dunn Parkway
Kodak, TN 37764
800-528-1234 ▪ (423) 933-3467

Room Rates:	$40–$100, including continental breakfast. AAA and AARP discounts.
Pet Charges or Deposits:	$5–$10 per day.
Rated: 3 Paws 🐾🐾🐾	82 rooms with king- or queen-sized beds, in-room cable television, some rooms with private balconies and hot tubs, a heated pool and kiddie pools, restaurant next door and a two-bedroom cottage.

Not far from the splendor and breathtaking views of the Great Smoky Mountains is the Dumplin Valley Inn. Nestled in the quiet country atmosphere of the historic Dumplin Valley, the inn offers guests spacious, tastefully decorated rooms with king- or queen-sized beds. Some rooms have private hot tubs and balconies overlooking scenic mountain views. For those wishing to have truly private accommodations for up to eight people, there is also a fully appointed two-bedroom cottage.

Guests are invited to start their day off with a complimentary continental breakfast before heading out for a busy day of sightseeing or to explore nearby Dollywood or the natural wonders of the Great Smoky Mountains National Park. For those who wish to spend some time relaxing at the inn, the heated pool is the perfect place for guests to lounge or take a swim while the youngsters frolic in the kiddie pool.

Snapp Inn Bed and Breakfast

Snapp Inn Bed and Breakfast
1990 Davy Crockett Park Road
Limestone, TN 37681
(423) 257-2482

Room Rates:	$55–$65, including full breakfast.
Pet Charges or Deposits:	None. Manager's approval required.
Rated: 3 Paws 🐾🐾🐾	2 guest rooms with private baths, fireplaces, refrigerators, cable TV, air conditioning, laundry facilities, barbecue grill, library, pool table and games.

I f you are looking for a relaxing, country atmosphere, the Snapp Inn Bed and Breakfast has that and more. Located in the farm country of the scenic Smoky Mountains, this 1815 Federal-style inn is decorated throughout in period antiques, including a rare Victorian reed organ. The large living room invites guests to relax and watch a movie on the VCR, or join others for engaging conversation. The large dining room is the setting for a full country breakfast—a delicious way to start the day.

The countryside is perfect for an outing or two; venture out and spend the day exploring the surrounding area with its babbling creeks and breathtaking mountain landscape. Or head out to the local park, within walking distance of the inn, for a picnic and a game of catch with the dog. The inn is only a short drive from many historical sights, canoeing, hiking, swimming and recreational areas.

Shoney's Inn

Shoney's Inn
508 Sunnyside Heights
McMinnville, TN 37110
800-222-2222 ▪ (615) 473-4446

Room Rates:	$42–$54, including continental breakfast. AAA and AARP discounts.
Pet Charges or Deposits:	None. Pets up to 30 lbs.
Rated: 3 Paws 🐾🐾🐾	61 guest rooms with free in-room movies and cable television, some rooms with coffee makers, microwaves and refrigerators, guest laundry services, swimming pool, Shoney's restaurant next door.

Conveniently located near several area attractions, state parks, lakes and recreational areas is the comfortable Shoney's Inn. Accommodations are handsomely furnished to make your surroundings as homey as possible. Enjoy a complimentary breakfast and newspaper each morning.

Pets and their owners alike will appreciate the spacious grounds surrounding the inn, where you can enjoy a leisurely stroll. The inn's crystal clear pool is an option, too, for on-site recreation.

Don't forget to visit one of the many parks and lakes in the area, such as Rock Island State Park and Fall Creek State Park, where dogs are welcome. Other notable attractions include five major lakes, shopping malls and crafts boutiques, the Savage Gulf Wilderness area, Indian excavation sites and Cumberland Caverns, the country's second-largest cave.

La Quinta Inn – Memphis East

La Quinta Inn – Memphis East
6068 Macon Cove
Memphis, TN 38134
800-531-5900 ▪ (901) 382-2323

Room Rates:	$61–$68, including continental breakfast. AAA and AARP discounts.
Pet Charges or Deposits:	None. Small pets only.
Rated: 3 Paws 🐾🐾🐾	128 rooms and 2 suites, all with large bathrooms, in-room coffee makers, alarm clocks, king-sized beds, cable television, entertainment system with first-run movies and video games, 24-hour front desk service, laundry and dry cleaning service, swimming pool, workout privileges at a nearby health club and non-smoking rooms.

Whether you are traveling on a business trip, a weekend getaway or an extended vacation, La Quinta Inn offers guests spacious, comfortable rooms with all the amenities required for an enjoyable stay. Kids of all ages will enjoy the latest video games and in-room, first-run movies, viewed on the expanded entertainment system. The spacious grounds are beautifully landscaped.

Included in the affordable price of your accommodations is a complimentary light breakfast, featuring your choice of cereal, fresh fruit, bagels, pastries, juice, milk and coffee. Fitness-minded travelers may use the workout privileges at a nearby health club.

Holiday Inn – Holidome

Holiday Inn – Holidome
2227 Old Fort Parkway
Murfreesboro, TN 37129
(615) 896-2420

Room Rates:	$59–$99. AAA, AARP, AKC and ABA discounts.
Pet Charges or Deposits:	None.
Rated: 3 Paws ❧ ❧ ❧	179 rooms with coffee makers, smoking and non-smoking rooms, fitness center, sauna, whirlpool, heated pool, Jacuzzi, laundry facilities, two restaurants and cocktail lounge.

Located in the city of Murfreesboro, the geographic center of the state and Tennessee's capital from 1819 to 1825, is the Holiday Inn – Holidome. Here guests will find modern, spacious rooms with in-room coffee makers, cable television with premium movie channels, dry cleaning and guest laundry services. Almost everyone will enjoy the Holidome Indoor Recreation Center, where you may test your skills in the game room, relax in the sauna or whirlpool or work out in the exercise room.

Venture out to one of the many historical sites, such as the Rutherford County Courthouse on East Main Street, the site of a dawn attack by General Nathan Bedford Forrest and his Confederate cavalry on Union troops camped within.

For your dining pleasure, the Patio Café serves up tasty sandwiches and snacks. Try Murfree's Table for a romantic evening of seafood, pasta, Tennessee catfish or ribs. For fun and an outrageously good time in the evening, stop by and share a toast and a tune in Conrad's Lounge.

Shoney's Inn

Shoney's Inn
2420 Music Valley Drive
Nashville, TN 37214
800-222-2222 ▪ (615) 885-4030

Room Rates:	$90–$139, including continental breakfast. AAA and AARP discounts.
Pet Charges or Deposits:	$100 refundable deposit. Small pets only. Complimentary pet treats.
Rated: 4 Paws ❦❦❦❦	172 large rooms and 13 suites with in-room coffee makers, free movies, cable television, heated indoor pool, whirlpool, valet laundry and airport transportation.

Set in the heart of the Music Valley area of Nashville, a favorite vacation destination is Shoney's Inn. A stone's throw from the world-famous attractions, activities and excitement of Nashville, accommodations are color-coordinated with a blend of muted blues, pinks, grape and teal; elegant wallpaper; handsome furnishings; and eye-catching artwork.

Your pets will appreciate friendly attention, as well as the special treats sent to the room, and pet exercise areas are available on site.

After a busy day of sightseeing and local adventures—maybe at Opryland or on a cruise down the Cumberland River aboard the General Jackson showboat—relax by (or in) the pool or enjoy a luxurious soak in the outdoor Jacuzzi. The inn's lounge is an intimate place to gather for a cocktail before heading out for a night on the town, or simply hang around and enjoy the live entertainment on tap at the inn.

Union Station Hotel

Union Station Hotel
1001 Broadway
Nashville, Tennessee 37203
800-331-2123 ▪ (615) 726-1001

Room Rates: $129–$165
Pet Charges or Deposits: None. Pets under 25 lbs. Manager's approval required.
Rated: 5 Paws 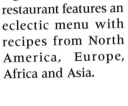 124 rooms with cable television, some refrigerators,
2 restaurants, cocktails, laundry service, area transportation
and valet parking.

Built at the height of Nashville's social and economic growth, the Union Station Hotel is a landmark in the heart of Music City and has earned a place on the National Register of Historic Places.

Originally opened in 1900 as a train station, the building now features a modern lobby with a stained-glass skylight, silvered mirrors, bas-relief artwork with gold trim and a black marble fountain. The barrel-vaulted ceiling has original stained-glass panels. A classic example of Romanesque-Revival architecture, the hotel is a limestone building with a massive clock tower and guest rooms with 22-foot-high ceilings.

Over the past 16 years, Arthur's Restaurant has been serving up award-winning meals to Nashvillians, as well as celebrities, journalists, government dignitaries and business leaders from around the nation and the world. The restaurant features an eclectic menu with recipes from North America, Europe, Africa and Asia.

The Heartlander Country Resort

The Heartlander Country Resort
2385 Parkway
Pigeon Forge, TN 37863
800-843-6686 ▪ (423) 453-4106

Room Rates:	$25–$120, including continental breakfast.
Pet Charges or Deposits:	$20 per stay.
Rated: 3 Paws 🐾🐾🐾	160 spacious guest rooms with private balconies, cable televisions with remote control, indoor and outdoor swimming pools.

Nestled in the foothills of the beautiful Smoky Mountains at the north entrance to Pigeon Forge, near Gatlinburg and the Great Smoky Mountains National Park, is the Heartlander Country Resort. Here guests will find spacious, comfortable rooms with private balconies offering mountain views from many rooms, plus indoor and outdoor swimming pools for year-round recreation.

The expansive grounds are perfect for you and your dog to take a nice long walk before heading out for a day of fun and activities in Pigeon Forge or one of the surrounding areas. Whether you spend your time visiting the Dollywood theme park, exploring the more than 500,000 acres and various hiking trails of the Great Smoky Mountains National Park, or relaxing with a delicious picnic lunch, you will appreciate coming back to the comforts of the Heartlander Country Resort.

Smokey Ridge Chalet and Cabin Rentals

Smokey Ridge Chalet and Cabin Rentals
2225 Parkway, Suite 1
Pigeon Forge, TN 37868
800-634-5814 ▪ (423) 428-5427

Room Rates:	$85–$150. Weekly and group rates available.
Pet Charges or Deposits:	Call for fees and deposit requirements. Manager's approval required.
Rated: 4 Paws 🐾🐾🐾🐾	60 individual chalets and cabins that sleep up to 12 people, with full kitchens, complete with linens and towels, color televisions, some with VCRs, fireplaces, Jacuzzis, pool.

I f you are looking for a home away from home for your next vacation, Smokey Ridge Chalet and Cabin Rentals has fully furnished chalets and log cabins with complete kitchens and all your linens provided. Choose from accommodations with one to five bedrooms and one to three bathrooms; built over a running stream or nestled on a ridge with beautiful views of the Smoky Mountains. Most rooms offer wood-burning fireplaces, perfect for an intimate evening or a cozy place to snuggle up with a good book.

There are plenty of activities to keep you busy in the area. Pigeon Forge offers the Dollywood theme park featuring homespun fun and traditions of the Smoky Mountains. The Dixie Stampede presents a program of music, comedy rodeo and Wild West-style performances. Then, of course, there's the Great Smoky Mountain National Park with more than 520,000 acres of natural landscape for picnicking, hiking and fishing.

Little Round Top Cabins

Little Round Top Cabins
3319 Mountain Lakes Way
Sevierville, TN 37862
(423) 428-5984

Room Rates:	$100–$140; weekly rates available.
Pet Charges or Deposits:	None. Small pets only. Must bring carrier to confine pet when not in room. Manager's approval required.
Rated: 5 Paws 🐾🐾🐾🐾🐾	7 cabins with 2–5 bedrooms, king- and queen-sized beds, whirlpools and hot tubs, satellite TV, wood-burning fireplaces, laundry facilities, full kitchens, central air and heat, gas barbecue grills, porches with rockers, all on 32 acres of private mountain.

Set amid 32 breathtaking acres of the scenic Wears Valley, between Townsend and Pigeon Forge, bordered by the Great Smoky Mountains National Park, are the Little Round Top Cabins. These charming, fully furnished cabins feature two to five bedrooms, with two or three bathrooms, fully equipped kitchens, wood-burning stone fireplaces with firewood supplied, large decks with gas barbecue grills and rocking chairs, laundry facilities in the cabins, whirlpool tubs and satellite television. Everything is furnished for you, including linens and towels. The fully stocked kitchens are complete with microwaves, toasters and a coffee makers.

Start your day off with a brisk hike through the hills, which are covered with mountain laurel, rhododendron, hemlock, numerous types of hardwood trees and large varieties of wildlife. Spectacular mountain views abound.

There are also plenty of attractions and shops to explore in the neighboring towns, as well as fishing, horseback riding, river rafting and golf.

Quality Inn

Quality Inn
1421 Murray's Chapel Drive
Sweetwater, TN 37874
800-647-3529 ▪ (423) 337-3541

Room Rates:	$45–$68. AAA, AARP, AKC and ABA discounts.
Pet Charges or Deposits:	None. Small pets only.
Rated: 3 Paws 🐾🐾🐾	145 guest rooms and 5 suites with cable television, movies, coffee makers, kitchens and refrigerators, indoor heated pool, whirlpool, dining room, valet laundry service, 2 adjacent restaurants.

Nestled in the foothills of the Great Smoky Mountains, near the gateway to the Cherokee National Forest, you'll find the Quality Inn – Sweetwater. The amenities of this welcoming inn include rooms with the convenience of kitchens, with coffee makers, refrigerators, radios, cable television with free in-room movies and valet laundry service.

Since the inn is located halfway between Knoxville and Chattanooga, you may want to strike out for a day of sightseeing. Of course, being near the Smoky Mountains and the Cherokee National Forest, you and your dog may want to explore the peaceful valleys and the roads less traveled in these naturally beautiful areas. If you want to stay on site, the pool area is a wonderful place to relax with a good book and a glass of iced tea.

Carnes' Log Cabin Rentals

Carnes' Log Cabin Rentals
PO Box 153
Townsend, TN 37882
(423) 448-1021

Room Rates:	$85–$115
Pet Charges or Deposits:	$10 per day: $50 deposit. Small pets only. Manager's approval required.
Rated: 5 Paws 🐾🐾🐾🐾🐾	7 furnished log cabins with king-sized beds, fully equipped kitchens, stone fireplaces, large covered porches with rocking chairs and swings, Jacuzzis, private outdoor hot tubs, cable TV with VCR, central air and heat, all linens and towels provided.

L ooking for the perfect Smoky Mountain getaway? Carnes' Log Cabins offers a peaceful alternative to traditional accommodations. Nestled in the secluded wooded setting are completely furnished, private cabins that blend rustic charm with modern conveniences such as fully equipped kitchens, full baths, stone fireplaces, private outdoor hot tubs, central air and heat, with all your linens and towels provided.

The cabins are only one mile from the entrance to the Great Smoky Mountains National Park and mere steps from the Little River, one of the nation's purest watersheds, where you and your dog can roam the five-mile stretch of river, try your luck at some of the fishing holes or go tubing and swimming. Just a short drive over the hill lies Gatlinburg, Pigeon Forge and Dollywood.

The large front porch, with its rocking chairs and swings, is the perfect place to relax after a busy or a not-so-busy day.

Goode Night Vacation Rentals

Goode Night Vacation Rentals
PO Box 322
Townsend, TN 37882
(423) 448-6842

Room Rates:	$85
Pet Charges or Deposits:	Call for deposit amount. Manager's approval required.
Rated: 3 Paws 🐾🐾🐾	6 cabins with kitchens, full baths, separate living rooms, most with fireplaces, decks, cable television; some with Jacuzzi.

Delightful vacation chalets can be found nestled in the wooded Smoky Mountains near the Great Smoky Mountain National Park and the Little River. They are offered by Goode Night Vacation Rentals. The secluded setting is perfect for a weekend getaway or a longer vacation.

Here await six charming cabins, including the peaceful Cedar cabin with lots of open space and an outdoor hot tub for six. The whimsical Treetops cabin is tucked into a wooded mountain setting and has an extra outdoorsy feeling. The Smoky Sunrise has a deck with wonderful views and all the comforts of home. The River Treasure is a cozy log cabin on five acres of meadows bordering the Little River; a perfect retreat for you and your dog. The Hillcrest is cozy and bright and perched in a wooded setting at the national park entrance and within walking distance of the river. This cabin can be rented as one large cabin or split up as two separate accommodations. Whichever you choose, you will find large bedrooms, full baths, separate living room areas, fireplaces, beautiful views and a garden with a Jacuzzi.

Hideaway Cottages and Log Cabins

Hideaway Cottages and Log Cabins
Cabins located in Townsend
Mailing address:
102 Oriole Lane
Marysville, TN 37803
(423) 984-1700

Room Rates:	$75–$150
Pet Charges or Deposits:	$10–$20 per stay; $100 deposit. Manager's approval required.
Rated: 3 Paws ❀ ❀ ❀	7 cottages and cabins with 1 to 3 bedrooms, all linens provided, fully equipped kitchens, air conditioning, barbecues, picnic tables and wood-burning fireplaces, set on private wooded acreage.

The wondrous sights and sounds of the Smokies surround you at Hideaway Cottages and Log Cabins. The seclusion and privacy of 30 densely wooded acres await you. The seven individual cabins and cottages are furnished, fully equipped accommodations ranging from 625 to 3,075 square feet, featuring wood-burning fireplaces, full kitchens, air conditioning, barbecues, picnic tables and decks.

Sit back, relax and let the peace and quiet transport you to a simpler time. Experience the quaintness of a pioneer cabin set on its own private acreage, while still enjoying the modern conveniences. Whether you spend your day taking in one of the local attractions, browsing through the antique and gift shops, marveling at the wonders of nature in one of the many nearby national parks, playing down by the creek in the five-acre meadow or heading to the Little River for a day of adventure with your dog, you will appreciate the peace and quiet of your secluded accommodations when you return.

Mountain Laurel Cabins

Mountain Laurel Cabins
146 Black Marsh Hollow Road
Townsend, TN 37882
(423) 448-9657

Room Rates: $95
Pet Charges or Deposits: $10 per stay. Call for deposit information.
Rated: 3 Paws 🐾🐾🐾   3 hand-hewn log cabins with full baths, complete kitchens with
                                dishwashers, central heat and air, ceiling fans, with some
                                fireplaces and whirlpool tubs.

J ust off Black Marsh Hollow Road in Townsend in the peaceful Smoky Mountains are the Mountain Laurel Cabins. Here you will find three hand-hewn log cabins with rustic appeal and modern amenities.

Choose from the Knight's Rest cabin, which will accommodate up to seven people in the three bedrooms and the sleeping loft. The homey Snuggle Down cabin has two full bedrooms and baths that will accommodate up to six people. The wide front porch is perfect for relaxing and enjoying nature. The Whippoorwill cabin is handicapped-accessible, offers a wrap-around porch, an open loft with two double beds, two bedrooms, a stone fireplace, a large whirlpool tub in the master bath and a cozy den with a wood-burning stove. This cabin sleeps eight and is ideal for two families or a large group to share.

The cabins are located near Gatlinburg, Pigeon Forge, Cades Cove and the Great Smoky Mountain National Park, so there are plenty of sights to see and places for you and your pet to explore.

Pearl's of the Mountains Cabin Rentals

Pearl's of the Mountains Cabin Rentals
7717 East Lamar Alexander Parkway
Townsend, TN 37882
800-324-8415 ▪ (423) 448-8801

Room Rates:	$70–$95
Pet Charges or Deposits:	$10 per stay. Manager's approval required.
Rated: 4 Paws 🐾🐾🐾🐾	3 cabins, each with fully equipped kitchen, microwave, dishwasher, laundry facilities, telephone, cable television, VCR, fireplace, large porches with swings and rockers, heating and air conditioning, charcoal grills, linens, towels, soaps and firewood.

L ocated in the Smoky Mountains near the Great Smoky Mountains National Park are the Pearl's of the Mountains Cabin Rentals. Here you will have the best views of the Smokies from your own private cabin. Choose a four-bedroom, two-level rental that sleeps from two to 10 people. It's perched high on a bluff overlooking the Little River, with lots of mature trees, making it a very private retreat. Stroll down to the river with the dog and wet your fishing line, have a picnic or go for a swim in the river.

Or you may choose a new two-bedroom cabin in the valley with spacious bedrooms which sleeps up to six people, has two private baths, a Jacuzzi and a large porch with rockers for relaxing. All cabins come fully equipped with towels, linens, soaps, firewood for the fireplace, cable television, VCRs, telephones, laundry facilities, heating, air conditioning, as well as kitchens with microwaves and dishwashers, making them an excellent choice for a private getaway.

Tuckaleechee Inn

Tuckaleechee Inn
160 Bear Lodge Drive
Townsend, TN 37882
800-487-6659 ▪ (423) 448-6442

Room Rates:	$70–$120, including full breakfast. Package rates available.
Pet Charges or Deposits:	$5 per day. Manager's approval required.
Rated: 4 Paws 🐾🐾🐾🐾	8 guest rooms, 2 large suites and 1 secluded cabin, all with private baths, air conditioning, some with Jacuzzis; common area with fireplace, exercise area for pets.

L ocated in the peaceful Smoky Mountains is the Tuckaleechee Inn. This authentic log cabin inn is the only one of its kind. Comfortable accommodations include two double beds and a private bath; some include a Jacuzzi. The common area with its cozy fireplace becomes an inviting gathering place for guests to converse or enjoy the satellite television. Nestled in the mountains, separate from the main inn, is a fully equipped, two-bedroom cabin that sleeps up to six guests. It is the perfect accommodation for those who want their privacy or for families.

Start your morning with a hearty breakfast and good conversation in the dining room before you head out for a day of adventure exploring the national parks, rafting on one of the nearby rivers, fishing in the streams, investigating the mysterious beauty of the local caverns or visiting the Dollywood theme park. Or for a day in low gear, you may just want to spend some time relaxing in a rocking chair with your dog at your feet, as you gaze out at the majestic views of the Smokies.

Twin Valley Ranch Bed and Breakfast Horse Ranch

Twin Valley Ranch Bed and Breakfast Horse Ranch
2848 Old Chihowee Road
Walland, TN 37886-2144
800-872-2235 ▪ (423) 984-0980

Room Rates:	$65–$85, including full breakfast. Vacation packages available.
Pet Charges or Deposits:	None. Manager's approval required. Horses welcome.
Rated: 4 Paws 🐾🐾🐾🐾	2 guest rooms and 1 cabin on a 260-acre horse ranch with homey accommodations, private cabins with kitchenette, full bath and deck. Horseback riding instructions and guided tours.

Wake up to the mountain's morning mist and breathtaking views at Twin Valley Ranch Bed and Breakfast Horse Ranch. Surrounded by tranquillity and simple country living, guests may choose to share the unique log home with its rustic log interior, two-story mountain stone fireplace and individually decorated rooms featuring special homey touches, or stay in the private log cabin nestled in the hills. The fully equipped cabin sleeps up to six people, offers a kitchenette, full bath and a sunny deck to enjoy the mountain views.

This mountain resort is a perfect place to bring your horse. The ranch has a grassy corral, complete with its own stream and shelter; or use one of the paddocks, with a shelter and running water. There are many trails throughout the scenic hills and valleys of this 260-acre ranch. You may arrange for a guided tour or head out on your own. When the stars come out, build a roaring campfire and breathe in the peace and quiet of nature.

Tennessee

Please Note: *Pets must be on a leash at all times and may be restricted to certain areas. For directions, use fees, pet charges and general information, contact the numbers listed below.*

National Parks

Great Smoky Mountains National Park encompasses 520,000 acres of parkland in both North Carolina and Tennessee. It is the largest protected land area east of the Rocky Mountains. Visitors will find camping facilities, picnic areas, hiking trails, fishing, nature programs and a visitors' center. For more information, call (423) 436-1200.

National Forest General Information

U.S. Forest Service
PO Box 2010
Cleveland, TN 37320

800 280-9700 – reservations
800 879-4496 – hearing impaired
(423) 476-9700

National Forests

CLEVELAND

Cherokee National Forest, in Eastern Tennessee near the city of Cleveland, is 630,000 acres of thickly forested, mountainous terrain punctuated by deep river gorges, streams and waterfalls. The area is dominated by species of pine, hemlock, oak and poplar trees. The park is divided into two sections by the Great Smoky Mountains National Park. There are 67 recreational areas, 715 miles of trails, including the Appalachian Trail, that traverse the forest. The Ocoee River offers white-water rafting trips. Visitors will find camping, picnic areas, hiking and biking trails, ramps for boating, boat rentals, fishing, swimming, nature programs and a visitors' center. For information, call (800) 250-8620 or (423) 772-3303.

National River and Recreation Areas

ONEIDA

Big South Fork National River and Recreation Area, located in northeastern Tennessee and southeastern Kentucky, consists of 115,000 acres of parkland with gorges carved through the Cumberland Plateau. There are natural arches, pinnacles, spires, sheer bluffs and huge rock overhangs. Visitors will also find 80 miles of streams for canoeing for skilled or beginner canoeists, back country camping facilities, picnic areas, hiking and bicycling trails, 300 miles of bridal trails, horse rentals, a ramp for boating, fishing, swimming, nature programs and a visitors' center. For more information, call (615) 879-3625.

Army Corps of Engineers

CELINA

Dale Hollow Lake, 3 miles east of Celina on SR 53, consists of 52,542 acres offering camping, picnic areas, hiking and biking trails, ramps for boating, boat rentals, fishing and swimming. For information, call (615) 736-7115.

DOVER

Lake Barkley, 50 miles north of Dover via SR 49, has 69,626 acres with camping, picnic areas, hiking trails, ramps for boating, boat rentals, fishing, swimming and a visitors center. For information, call (615) 736-7115.

NASHVILLE

Cheatham Lake, 25 miles west of Nashville on SR 12 and consists of 10,727 acres offering visitors camping, picnic areas, hiking trails, ramps for boating, boat rentals, fishing and swimming. For information, call (615) 736-7115.

Cordell Hull Lake, 50 miles east of Nashville off SR 85, is 32,705 acres of parkland with camping, picnic areas, hiking and biking trails, ramps for boating, boat rentals, fishing, swimming and a visitors' center. Call (615) 736-7115 for information.

J. Percy Priest Lake, 11 miles east off I-40, encompasses 14,200 acres and offers camping, picnicking, hiking and biking trails, ramps for boating, boat rentals, fishing, swimming and a visitors' center. Call (615) 736-7115 for information.

Old Hickory Reservoir, 15 miles northeast of Nashville via US 31E, consists of 22,500 acres with camping, picnicking, hiking trails, a boat ramp, boat rentals, fishing, swimming and a visitors' center. For information, call (615) 736-7115.

State Park General Information

Tennessee State Parks
Seventh Floor, L & C Tower
401 Church Street
Nashville, TN 37243-0446

(800) 421-6683 – reservations
(615) 532-0001 – information

State Parks

CAMDEN

Nathan Bedford Forrest State Park, 7 miles northeast of Camden via Eva Road, leading off the east side of the courthouse square, consists of 840 acres offering camping, picnic areas, hiking trails, ramps for boating, fishing, swimming, nature programs and a visitors' center.

CARYVILLE

Cove Lake State Park, located 1 mile north of Caryville off US 25W, consists of 1,500 acres of parkland with camping, picnic areas, hiking and biking trails, boating, boat rentals, fishing, swimming and a visitors' center.

CHATTANOOGA

Harrison Bay State Park, located 10 miles northeast of Chattanooga off SR 58, consists of 1,300 acres of parkland with camping, picnic areas, hiking trails, ramps for boating, boat rentals, marina, fishing, swimming.

DICKSON

Montgomery Bell State Park, 8 miles east of Dickson on US 70, encompasses 4,600 acres of parkland for backpacking, golf, tennis, camping, picnicking, hiking, boating, boat rentals, fishing, swimming and nature program.

EASTVIEW

Big Hill Pond State Park, 10 miles west of Eastview on SR 57, consists of 5,028 acres and offers camping, picnic areas, hiking trails, boating, boat rentals, fishing, swimming, nature programs and a visitors' center.

ELIZABETHTON

Roan Mountain State Park, located 20 miles southeast of Elizabethton off US 19E via SR 143, consists of 2,000 scenic acres and offers visitors cross-country skiing, museum, camping, picnicking, hiking trails, fishing, swimming, nature programs and a visitors center.

MORRISTOWN

Panther Creek State Park, located 6 miles west of Morristown off US 11E, encompasses 1,290 acres and offers visitors camping, picnicking, hiking, a boat ramp, fishing and swimming.

NASHVILLE

Edgar Evins State Park, east of Nashville off I-40 on Center Hill Lake, consists of 6,000 acres offers camping, picnicking, hiking, ramps for boating, boat rentals and fishing.

NORRIS

Big Ridge State Park, 14 miles northeast of Norris on SR 61, has 3,600 acres of parkland with camping, picnicking, hiking, a ramp for boating, boat rentals, fishing, swimming, nature program and a visitors' center.

Norris Dam State Park, located in Norris consists of 2,400 acres and offers camping, picnicking, hiking, a ramp for boating, fishing, swimming, nature program and a visitors' center.

PARIS

Paris Landing State Park, located 16 miles northeast of paris on US 79, consists of 841 acres offering visitors, golf, tennis, marina, playground, camping picnicking, hiking, a ramp for boating, boat rentals, fishing, swimming and nature program.

PIKEVILLE

Fall Creek Falls State Park, located 14 miles northwest of Pikeville off SR 30, offers visitors backpacking, golf, tennis, camping, picnicking, hiking and biking trails, boating, boat rentals, fishing, swimming, nature program and a visitors' center.

ROCK ISLAND

Rock Island State Park, located at Rock Island off US 70S, consists of 350 acres offering visitors tennis, camping, picnicking, a ramp for boating, boat rentals, fishing and swimming

WARTBURG

Frozen Head State Park, located 6 miles east of Wartburg on SR 62, consists of 10,000 scenic acres offering visitors a playground, camping, picnicking, hiking and nature program.

HENDERSON

Chickasaw State park, located 7 miles west of Henderson on SR 100, consists of 11,215 acres and offers visitors horse rentals, camping, picnicking, hiking trails, boating, boat rentals, fishing and swimming.

HENNING

Fort Pillow State Park, 18 miles west of Henning off SR 87 via SR 207, encompasses 1,650 historic acres and offers camping, picnicking, hiking trails, a ramp for boating, fishing and a visitors' center.

JAMESTOWN

Pickett State Park, located 13 miles northeast of Jamestown on SR 154, with 14,000 acres of parkland offering backpacking, camping picnicking, hiking, ramps for boating, boat rentals, fishing and swimming.

KINGSPORT

Warrior's Path State Park, 5 miles southeast of Kingsport on US 23, has 1,500 acres of parkland with golf, horse rentals, a marina, camping, picnicking, hiking and biking trails, a ramp for boating, boat rentals, fishing, swimming and a nature program.

LEBANON

Cedars of Lebanon State Park, 8 miles south of Lebanon on US 231, has 8,900 acres offering camping, picnicking, hiking trails, swimming, a nature program and a visitors' center.

LEXINGTON

Natchez Trace State Park, 15 miles northeast of Lexington, consists of 46,000 acres and offers visitors tennis, camping, picnicking, hiking trails, a ramp for boating, boat rentals, fishing, swimming and a nature program.

MEMPHIS

Meeman-Shelby Forest, 16 miles north of Memphis off US 51, is a 12,512-acre park and offering horse rentals, camping, picnicking, hiking and biking trails, a ramp for boating, boat rentals, fishing, swimming, a nature program and a visitors' center.

MONTEAGLE

South Cumberland State Park, located 4.5 miles east on SR 56 from I-24 exit 134, consists of 8 separate areas in a 12,000-acre park with a playground, tennis, camping, picnicking, hiking, boating, fishing, swimming and a visitors' center.

Index

About the Author. . . from a dog's point of view

Dreamer Dawg, office manager and "cover girl" for Bon Vivant Press, is a nine-year-young Labrador Retriever. When not exploring the food and lodging for each regional book, you can find Dreamer relaxing onboard her boat in the Monterey harbor or running with the horses in the Salinas Valley.

Owners Robert & Kathleen Fish, authors of the popular "Secrets" series, have researched and written fifteen award-winning cookbooks and travel books, and are always on the lookout for lodgings with style and character.

Other titles in the Pets Welcome™ series are *Pets Welcome™ California, Pets Welcome™ Pacific Northwest, Pets Welcome™ New England* and *Pets Welcome™ Southwest.*

Bon Vivant Press

A division of The Millennium Publishing Group

PO Box 1994

Monterey, CA 93942

800-524-6826 • 408-373-0592 • 408-373-3567 FAX • Website: http://www.millpub.com

Send _____ copies of **Pets Welcome California** at $15.95 each.

Send _____ copies of **Pets Welcome America's South** at $15.95 each.

Send _____ copies of **Cooking With the Masters of Food & Wine** at $34.95 each.

Send _____ copies of **The Elegant Martini** at $17.95 each.

Send _____ copies of **Cooking Secrets From Around the World** at $15.95 each.

Send _____ copies of **Cooking Secrets From America's South** at $15.95 each.

Send _____ copies of **Louisiana Cooking Secrets** at $15.95 each.

Send _____ copies of **Pacific Northwest Cooking Secrets** at $15.95 each.

Send _____ copies of **Cooking Secrets for Healthy Living** at $15.95 each.

Send _____ copies of **The Great California Cookbook** at $14.95 each.

Send _____ copies of **The Gardener's Cookbook** at $15.95 each.

Send _____ copies of **The Great Vegetarian Cookbook** at $15.95 each.

Send _____ copies of **California Wine Country Cooking Secrets** at $14.95 each.

Send _____ copies of **San Francisco's Cooking Secrets** at $13.95 each.

Send _____ copies of **Monterey's Cooking Secrets** at $13.95 each.

Send _____ copies of **New England's Cooking Secrets** at $14.95 each.

Send _____ copies of **Cape Cod's Cooking Secrets** at $14.95 each.

Send _____ copies of **Jewish Cooking Secrets From Here and Far** at $14.95 each.

Add $4.50 postage and handling for the first book ordered and $1.50 for each additional book. Please add 7.25% sales tax per book, for those books shipped to California addresses.

Please charge my ☐ Visa   # _____
                 ☐ MasterCard

Expiration date _____ Signature _____

Enclosed is my check for _____

Name_____

Address _____

City_____ State _____ ZIP_____

☐ **This is a gift. Send directly to:**

    Name_____

    Address _____

    City_____ State _____ ZIP_____

☐ **Autographed by the author**

    Autographed to_____